W9-BUX-559

The Dust Bowl and the Depression in American History

Debra McArthur

Enslow Publishers, Inc.
40 Industrial Road
Box 398
Berkeley Heights, NJ 07922
USA

PO Box 38
Aldershot
Hants GU12 6BP
UK

http://www.enslow.com

Dedicated to the Dust Bowl survivors who so graciously shared their memories with me for this book

Library of Congress Cataloging-in-Publication Data

McArthur, Debra.
The dust bowl and the Depression in American history / Debra McArthur.
p. cm. — (In American history)
Includes bibliographical references (p. 118) and index.
ISBN 0-7660-1838-5
1. Dust storms—Great Plains—History—20th century—Juvenile literature.
2. Droughts—Great Plains—History—20th century—Juvenile literature.
3. Farmers—Great Plains—Social conditions—20th century—Juvenile literature. 4. Agriculture—Environmental aspects—Great Plains—History—20th century—Juvenile literature. 5. Agriculture—Social aspects—Great Plains—History—20th century—Juvenile literature. 6. Great Plains—History—20th century—Juvenile literature. 7. United States—Economic conditions—1918–1945—Juvenile literature. 8. Agriculture and state—United States—History—20th century—Juvenile literature. 9. Depressions—1929—United States—Juvenile literature. [1. Dust storms—Great Plains. 2. Droughts—Great Plains—History. 3. Agriculture—Great Plains—History. 4. Great Plains—History. 5. Depression—1929.] I. Title. II. Series.
E395 .M38 2002
978'.032—dc21

2001001377

Printed in the United States of America

10 9 8 7 6 5 4 3 2 1

To Our Readers: We have done our best to make sure all Internet addresses in this book were active and appropriate when we went to press. However, the author and the publisher have no control over and assume no liability for the material available on those Internet sites or on other Web sites they may link to. Any comments or suggestions can be sent by e-mail to comments@enslow.com or to the address on the back cover.

Illustration Credits: American Folklife Center, p 108. Courtesy of Missouri Town 1855, Jackson County Missouri Parks and Recreation, p. 15; Enslow Publishers, Inc., pp. 12, 30, 99; Farm Service Administration, p. 87; FDR Presidential Library, pp. 9, 33, 47, 65, 67, 70, 84, 107, 110; Kansas State Historical Society, pp. 14, 18, 45; Library of Congress, pp. 50, 56, 62, 71, 73, 74, 82, 92, 94; Natural Resources Conservation Service, United States Department of Agriculture, p. 90; Photo by Leslie P. Myers, p. 23; Used with permission of the Davis family, pp. 7, 16, 40.

Cover Illustration: Farm Service Administration; FDR Presidential Library; Library of Congress

★ Contents ★

Black Sunday

On the 14th day of April of 1935,
There struck the worst of dust storms that ever filled the sky.
You could see that dust storm coming, the cloud looked death-like black,
And through our mighty nation, it left a dreadful track.

Our relatives were huddled into their oil boom shacks,
And the children they was crying as it whistled through the cracks.
And the family it was crowded into their little room,
They thought the world had ended, and they thought it was their doom.[1]

—Woody Guthrie, "Dust Storm Disaster"

April 14, 1935, dawned clear and bright in Dodge City, Kansas. After nearly a month of dusty days, it was a welcome change. Although springtime in western Kansas had always included windy weather, the last three years had been miserable. Since the farmers took over the plains, the native grasses had been replaced by fields of wheat. A severe drought that had been going on since 1931 had killed most of the crops, leaving the top layer of soil exposed. The slightest breeze set the dirt in motion, creating huge dust storms, which became known as "black blizzards." A record number of dust storms had swept the countryside that spring.

After church that day, many adults made plans to do cleanup work. There was plenty to do. The latest dust storm had lasted four days. The powder-fine soil blown by the wind had come through every crevice around doors and windows. The storms always left a heavy coating of dust on everything in the house. Children were sent outside to play while their mothers swept the house and washed clothes. With the sunny morning and clear sky, no one could have suspected that this day would later be known as "Black Sunday."

Fear on the Horizon

By midafternoon, a change was in the air. The temperature began to drop, falling nearly fifty degrees in just a few hours. Chickens in barnyards ran nervously in circles. Hundreds of wild birds took to the air, screeching. Suddenly, on the horizon to the north, a huge black cloud seemed to boil up from the earth. It was moving swiftly toward town. People scrambled to find the nearest shelter as the familiar shout went through the streets: "Dust storm!"[2]

According to the *Dodge City Journal*, "many people, fearing a tornado, hurried to their cellars. Inky darkness followed. . . . Children who had left home to

Margaret Davis, who lived in Kansas during the time of Black Sunday, took this photo of the dust storm as it approached her family's farm in Syracuse.

play caused their parents several hours of anxiety until they were located. Traffic on all highways was halted."[3]

"The End of the World"

Fifteen-year-old Bob Beatty of Dodge City was driving his father's pickup truck that Sunday afternoon. He took several friends with him to do a little fishing. They had just arrived at a fishing spot on the Pawnee River, just north of Spearville, Kansas, when they saw the huge black cloud on the horizon to the north. The day turned instantly as dark as night, and the blowing dust stung their faces and throats. Bob's friend, Jonelle Bays, thought it was the end of the world. Twins Eilee and Eileen McCabe said, "We didn't know whether to start praying or running."[4]

The blinded teens made their way back to the pick-up truck, but the engine was choked with dirt and would not start. The girls crowded into the front seat, while Bob and the other boys huddled in the bed of the truck. Eilee cut strips of cloth from her trousers and gave them to her friends to use as face masks to help filter the dust so they could breathe. After thirty minutes passed without a break in the storm, Bob Beatty and Nelson Moore decided to leave the truck to seek help at a farmhouse they had passed. Unable to see the road, they crawled along the edge of it for over a quarter of a mile to the house. The farmer returned with the boys and helped the teenagers to safety at his house.[5]

Unnatural Darkness

The storm hit Rolla, Kansas, at about 4:00 P.M. that day. James R. Dickenson was just a baby at the time, but his mother and aunt later told him about that day. Like Jonelle Bays, James's mother, Anna Dickenson, thought it was surely the end of the world. James's aunt, Opal Dickenson, was coming home from church choir practice when the storm hit. "When I got home," she recalled, "I lit a coal oil lamp, and it was so dark you could hardly see it, even though it was the middle of the afternoon."[6]

In Meade, Kansas, the conditions were just as bad. The streetlights came on because of the sudden darkness. The dirt in the air was so thick that people could not see even a foot in front of their faces. One man was less than an eighth of a mile from his home when he lost his way. His family found him later, unconscious and barely alive, just a few yards from the house.[7]

Meanwhile, pilot Laura Ingalls (not related to author Laura Ingalls Wilder) was high above the ground, attempting to set a women's speed record for her coast-to-coast flight. She took off from Los Angeles, California, hoping to make it to New York in fifteen hours, in order to break pilot Amelia Earhart's record of seventeen hours. About six hours into her trip, she ran into the dust over the plains. "I was up 22,000 feet and it still was above me," she said. "It

The Black Sunday dust storm approaches Spearman, Texas.

was the most appalling thing I ever saw in all my years of flying." She estimated that she was over Wichita, Kansas, when she turned back. She landed safely in Alamosa, Colorado, after flying blind for nearly four hours.[8]

Barely Holding On

This was not the first of the dust storms, nor would it be the last, but many people said it was the worst. Lawrence Svobida was working hard to farm his land in Meade County, Kansas, despite the continuing drought and blowing soil. Although many of his neighbors were giving up and leaving their farms, Svobida wanted to stay. Still, his optimism was fading. He later described April 14, 1935, as "the blackest day within the memory of living man."[9]

What caused this horrible natural catastrophe? Some said it was the "Wrath of God." As it turned out, it was probably the farmers themselves.

THE GREAT AMERICAN DESERT

When President Thomas Jefferson negotiated the Louisiana Purchase in 1803, he had a grand idea in mind. He intended to expand the United States to include enough land so that every man could have a plot of ground to own and work. The new territory would include the land west of the Mississippi River to the eastern edge of the Rocky Mountains, except for present-day Texas and New Mexico. All he had to do was convince Congress to spend $15 million to buy it from France.

Jefferson believed that farming was the noblest occupation a person could have. "Cultivators of the earth are the most valuable citizens," he wrote. "They are the most vigorous, the most independent, the most virtuous, and they are tied to their country and wedded to its liberty and interests by the most lasting bonds."[1]

Zebulon Pike's Report

In 1806, United States Army Lieutenant Zebulon Pike was sent to explore the new territory and send

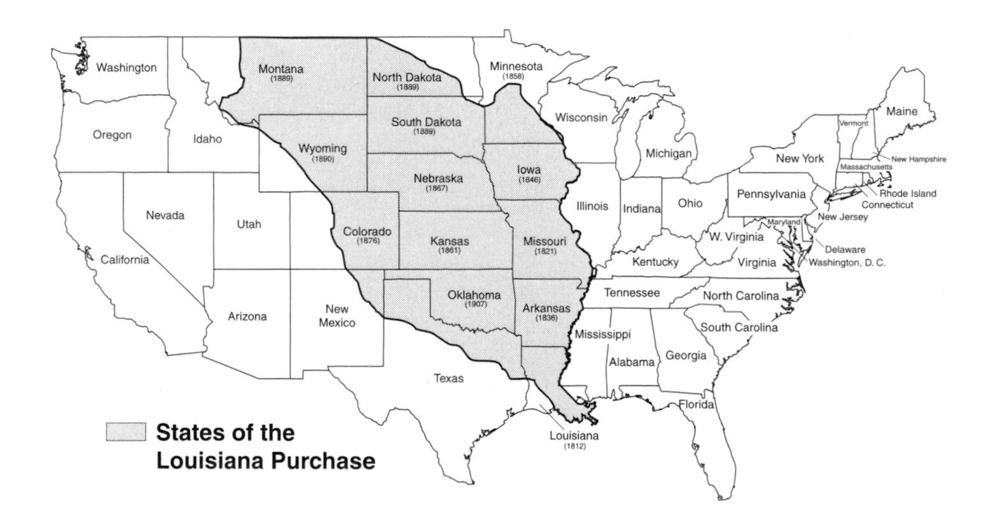

The 1803 Louisiana Purchase nearly doubled the size of the United States.

back a report. Pike was not as optimistic as Jefferson about the possibilities for settlers on the vast treeless plains. He referred to the area west of the 100th meridian as the continent's "internal desert," and described a land "where the wind had thrown up the sand in all the fanciful forms of the ocean's rolling wave, and on which not a speck of vegetable matter existed." He concluded that this area was "incapable of cultivation."[2] Pike's observations were soon picked up by mapmakers who identified the middle section of the continent as the "Great American Desert." Because of this idea, the land would remain largely untouched for several decades.

President Lincoln Signs the Homestead Act

The Homestead Act of 1862 opened up all the territory that was still in the public domain (owned by the government, but not by any individual). The act offered 160 acres of land to any person age twenty-one or older who was the head of a household. The homesteader had to be willing to build a home and farm the land for five years. The only cost was a filing fee of $10 and a $2 fee to the land agent. At the end of the five years, the homesteader went back to the land office, with two of his neighbors along to verify that he had farmed and improved the land, and $6 in his pocket to pay for the patent, or title. He then received the title for the property, which was signed by the current president of the United States. Many people joined the rush to claim land in the territory west

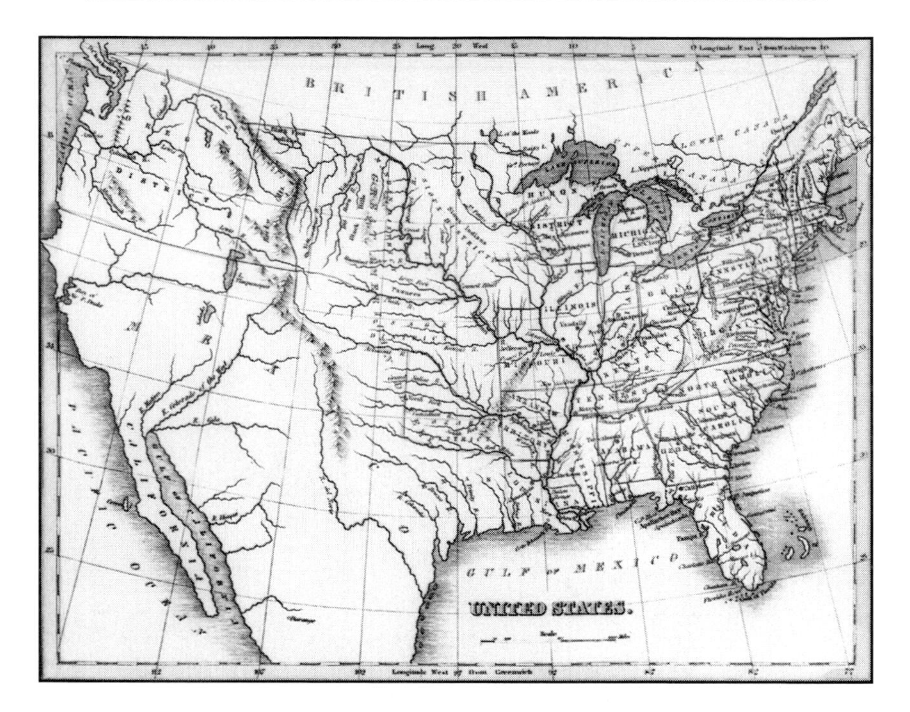

This map from 1835 shows the inscription "Great American Desert" printed along the 100th meridian line.

of Missouri, and the population of the eastern edges of the Plains grew quickly.

Sodbusting

Farming was never easy, though. The settlers faced a huge job before they could even begin to farm: They had to break through the tough prairie sod in order to get to the farmable soil beneath it. Most settlers traveled west in their covered wagons with just the bare essentials: a few household goods, some cornmeal and other food items, a horse or ox, a cow, and most importantly, a "sodbusting" plow.

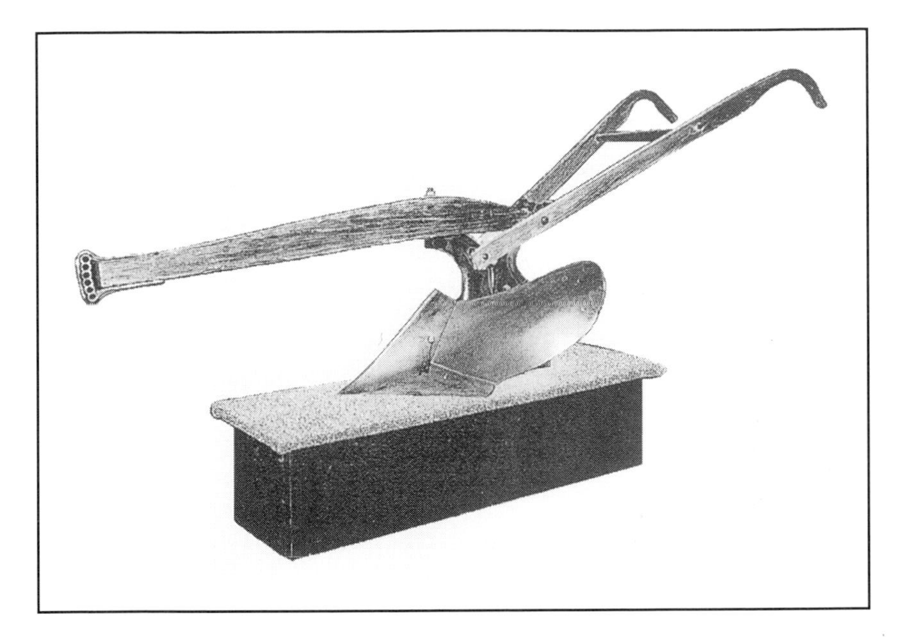

A plow similar to this one would be a necessity for homesteaders headed to the southern Plains in order to break through the tough prairie sod.

The roots of the prairie grass were tough and deep from centuries of growth. A strong team of horses or oxen pulling a sodbusting plow could cut through the top layer of roots and soil—the sod—but it was hard, slow work. Once he had made cuts, the farmer could peel back the sod, which was several inches thick. The roots and soil would cling together and could be peeled up off the ground, leaving the rich, moist soil underneath exposed.

Soddies

Building a house was a challenge on the prairie. Wood was scarce and expensive, so pioneers learned to use

H. M. Davis on his farmstead near Syracuse, Kansas, in 1912. The sod house in the background was the family's first home.

the most abundant material they had: sod. Because it clung together so well, farmers would cut strips of sod with a special plow called a "grasshopper" to use as building material. They stacked the sod like bricks to form the walls of houses and barns. These became known as "soddies." The roof was usually made of more strips of sod. It worked well, for the most part, at least until it rained. The rain would drip through the roof, turning the dirt floor into mud. Although the earthen walls kept out the constant wind and insulated well against the cold and the summer heat, the soddy was dark and damp year-round.[3]

A Little of Everything

Besides a cash crop like corn or wheat, most family farms also had large gardens to provide vegetables for the family to eat and to sell. Most farm wives prepared fresh produce in the growing season and also preserved vegetables and fruits in jars for use by the family in the winter. Many were also able to sell extra canned goods at market.

Another important source of food and income for farm families was livestock such as hogs and chickens. These animals could be fed leftover grain and vegetables, thus costing the family very little. Pork could be cured to preserve it without refrigeration. Chickens provided eggs in all seasons, as well as fresh meat. Most farm families could raise enough chickens and hogs to feed their own families and also to sell for additional income.

Still, making a living on a farm on the Great Plains was difficult. Nature often played tricks. Grasshoppers, hail, or a tornado could wipe out a year's work in a day. Farming was always a battle against the elements, but the settlers who were hardy and determined found that they could make a home and a living in this area. Reverend Olof Olsson arrived in Kansas with other Swedish immigrants in 1869. In a letter to a friend in Sweden, he wrote, "We do not dig gold with pocket knives . . . but what we aim at is to own our own homes, where each one has his own property, which with God's blessings will provide him with the sustenance which he and his family need." [4]

Drought and Dust

The hardest element to overcome was the cycle of drought. Farmers expected a year of drought every six or seven years. Still, the years between usually provided just enough rain to get by, with an occasional year of very good moisture, which would produce a larger crop than usual. Because of the many different types of crops and products they produced, most farmers did not need to worry much about occasional problems. This diversification meant that farm families would be able to survive even a year of drought, grasshoppers, tornadoes, or hail.

Although the Homestead Act of 1862 invited settlers to the open prairie, most were reluctant to go too

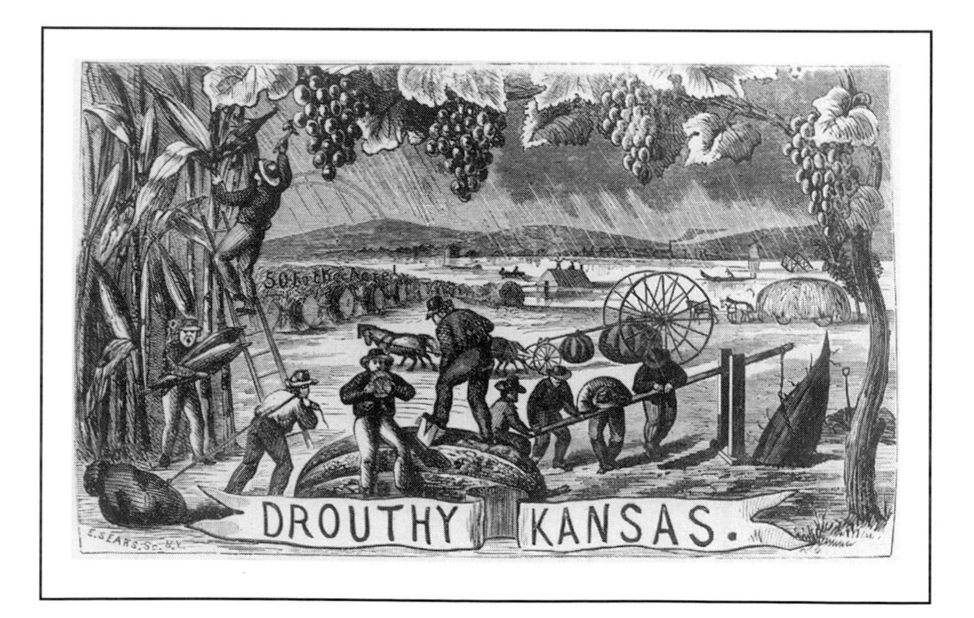

This cartoon entitled "Drouthy Kansas" was drawn in response to criticism that Kansas was too dry to farm.

far west. They still believed that the land of the Southern Plains (present-day Kansas, Oklahoma, Texas, New Mexico, and eastern Colorado) was too dry to farm. Besides, most settlers found good land along the trails before they got too far west. It would still be twenty years before many farmers ventured much farther westward than Dodge City, Kansas.[5]

Cattle Drives

Cattlemen next took over the Plains. After the Civil War, they began to drive their herds north out of Texas to markets along the railroad lines in Missouri and later as far as New Mexico and Wyoming. As the cattle walked along, they ate the rich (and free) prairie grass and fattened themselves all the way to market.

Once the ranchers saw how much money they could make from the cattle, they continued to drive more and more animals across the Plains. The grasses could not keep up. In 1870, it had taken only five acres of grass to fatten a steer; by 1880, the grass had thinned so much that it took fifty acres of grass to fatten a steer for market.[6]

The next herds to graze the Plains were sheep, and they were even more destructive. The leafy blades of grass grow from the part of the plant where the roots join the stem. This growth nub is just above the surface of the soil. The physical structure of a sheep's mouth, its split lip, allows it to eat the grass all the way down to the ground, below the growth nub. When severe cold hit in the winter of 1886, the grass did not survive and millions of head of cattle and sheep died. The once-rich Texas cattle ranchers lost their fortunes and abandoned the Plains. By now, much of the grass was gone, and soil began to blow. It was a warning that people did not take seriously.[7]

Back to the Plow

About the time the cattle left, the farmers arrived. The railroad companies advertised the plains and brought thousands of settlers west of the 100th meridian from the Dakotas to Oklahoma. In 1880, the area west of Dodge City, Kansas, was mostly unsettled. By 1885, settlers were arriving daily by train to stake a claim in the areas west of Dodge City and east of the Rocky Mountains before all the land was taken. Soddies now dotted the western Plains. Settlers were eager to make their fortunes in this land, which was now being called "The Last Frontier." By 1890, 6 million people lived on the Great Plains, more than double the population of 1880.[8]

Unfortunately, many of the new farmers came expecting land that was easy to farm. The dry, hot climate did not produce the yield they were used to on land farther east. Their 160-acre farms could not produce enough grain to support a family, even in years when the rainfall was above average. The homesteaders had expected to become rich but were barely making a living.

When the cycle of drought came around again in 1889–1895, it was more than most of the new settlers

SOURCE DOCUMENT

SEPTEMBER 11, 1869. THE FURTHER I CAME INTO THE WEST, THE MORE PLEASANT I FOUND IT. THE WEST IS BEST FOR THE PERSON WHO IS SEEKING A HOME. THE EAST'S LARGE CITIES OFFER A RICH FIELD FOR CLEVER MONEY LOVERS. THE WEST WITH ITS LARGE STRETCHES OF FERTILE, UNCLAIMED LAND IS A RICH FIELD FOR THE INDUSTRIOUS FARMER, WHO IS NOT AFRAID IN THE EARLY YEARS TO SUBJECT HIMSELF TO TOIL AND DIFFICULTIES.[9]

This letter was written by the Reverend Olaf Olsson, a Kansas settler, to C. W. Weinberg in Sweden.

could take. Many of them packed up their belongings and headed back where they had come from. They had not established any real ties to the land or their communities, and they had not stayed long. The population decreased, back to near what it had been before 1880.

More Cattle Ranching

Those who had not yet been on their land five years abandoned it, and it went back to government ownership. Those who owned their land sold out to cattle ranchers for whatever price they could get. The ranchers were able to buy farms for very low prices from bankrupt farmers, but they now realized that their profits were directly related to the condition of the grass. They did not overgraze it as much as the earlier cattle drivers had, but it was still hard to make much profit from the small plots of land.

One More Chance for Farmers

By 1910, several important changes brought farmers back to the Plains. Convinced of the difficulty of making a living on the 160-acre farms, Congress passed the Enlarged Homestead Act in 1909. It doubled the size of a homestead that could be obtained from the government. Three years later, the residency requirement to gain ownership decreased from five to only three years. The federal government began to advertise the Plains as a profitable place to farm, and the settlers returned.

An important development at this time was a new type of farming known as "dry farming." With this method, a farmer could plow his fields and plant winter wheat in the fall. The plants emerged in the late winter and grew through the spring. After harvest in midsummer, farmers left the fields covered with the stubble of the harvested plants to retain moisture and keep the dirt from blowing.

The years that followed were good ones for farmers. For three years in a row—1914, 1915, and 1916—the Plains had above-average rainfall. It was a lucky break for the farmers. For years, the saying "rain follows the plow" had led farmers to believe that if they only put the work into the land, nature would repay them generously. Now it certainly seemed true.

New Machines

Perhaps the biggest contributor to the growth of farming was the invention and use of new farming equipment. Mechanization of farming meant that one farmer could now work more land without having to hire much help. Also, unlike teams of animals, tractors did not have to rest. James Dickenson's uncle in Morton County, Kansas, was among the farmers who were breaking sod as fast as they could make their new machines work, both day and night: "Uncle Dean recalled long hours on the tractor and how he and others tied themselves to the tractor seat with a length of rope in case they dozed off."[10] According to Dickenson, 13.5 million new acres, including about 11 million acres of native prairie grass were plowed up to make room for wheat during the years 1914–1919.[11]

Steam-powered tractors helped farmers cultivate larger farms with fewer laborers in the 1910s. By the 1920s, gasoline-powered tractors made farming still easier.

Gasoline supplied the energy they needed, so the farmer no longer needed grazing land. He could now farm all his acreage. Even though the amount of wheat produced per acre was still below that of the eastern states, large-scale farming could now be profitable, because the labor hours needed to produce the wheat were going down. This meant that a farmer could produce more wheat with fewer hours of work and fewer people needed to do the work. In 1830, it had required about two hundred fifty to three hundred hours of labor to produce one hundred bushels of wheat using the kind of hand and horse-drawn tools the pioneers had. With gasoline-powered tractors and trucks, by 1930, it required only fifteen to twenty labor hours to produce the same amount of wheat.[12]

World War I caused great shortages of food in Europe and increased the demand for farm products from the United States, especially wheat. It was now more profitable for farmers to plant all their land in one crop than to have the diversified farms of fifty years earlier. The prices paid for grain during World War I rose to levels never seen before. In 1914, a farmer could sell his wheat at the rate of $0.93 a bushel. By 1919, the price was above $2.30 per bushel.[13] Even though the prices did drop again during the 1920s, production was so high that most farmers were still making enough money to cover their costs and continue to buy more machinery.

Perhaps the farmer had finally conquered the "Great American Desert."

3

Drought and Depression Set In

As the 1920s ended and the 1930s began, the Plains states farmers were becoming more and more successful. As farmers increased the number of machines on their farms, they were harvesting more than ever before. Now, almost all farmers were growing only wheat, and they were growing more of it than ever. Near the end of the 1920s, farmers in Kansas were averaging about thirteen bushels of wheat per acre.[1] Farmers in other states were harvesting similar amounts. The Southern Plains became known as the "bread basket" of America.

Machines and Money

Of course, machinery was a big investment for farmers, but most felt they needed the equipment in order to save on labor costs and produce enough grain to make a profit. By the end of the 1920s, the railroads were bringing about five times as much farm equipment into the Plains as they had just five years earlier.

A typical farmer in 1930 would need a truck, a tractor, and a combine (a machine that would harvest the wheat and also separate the seeds from the rest of the plant).

Many farmers did not have enough money to buy the machinery they needed. Some could get money from a bank by taking out a loan. Some farmers used their own farms as collateral for the loan. By doing this, a farmer agreed to give the ownership of his land to the bank if he could not repay the loan. In some cases, the dealers who sold the machinery would give a farmer credit so that he could make payments on the machinery he needed over time rather than paying all at once.

Considering the cost of these machines, the gas to run them, and his seeds and fertilizer, a farmer would spend about four dollars per acre on production. At this rate, he would need to harvest about ten bushels of wheat per acre and then sell the wheat at forty cents per bushel in order to make just enough to cover his costs.[2] With production averaging 13 bushels per acre and selling for $1.03, most farmers were doing well.[3] As long as production and prices remained high, they knew they would have no trouble paying off their debts.

Hard Times in America

Not everyone in the United States was doing as well as the farmers, however. In October 1929, the stock market crashed, marking the beginning of the Great

Depression. When people buy stocks, they buy shares or small pieces of businesses or goods. Just before the crash, people were buying shares even when they did not have the money to pay for them. They made a small down payment, then borrowed the rest of the money. They gambled that their stocks would increase in value. If so, the investor could pay back the loan and make a profit by selling the shares at the new higher price.

In October 1929, some investors got worried and began selling their stocks. Others, wanting to get out while the prices were still high, did the same. Within a few days, nearly everyone wanted to sell, no one wanted to buy, and stocks became worthless. Businesses and wealthy investors lost millions of dollars, and investors who were not wealthy lost everything they had. Newspapers ran stories about Wall Street investors who had lost everything committing suicide by jumping from the windows of skyscrapers.

Banks that had lent money for the purchase of stocks had no way to collect the loans. By July 1930, 640 banks had closed, and the customers of those banks lost the money they had deposited in them. The next year, 1,553 more banks closed. Businesses and factories also closed, and workers lost their jobs. By 1931, nearly 8 million people, over 16 percent of the labor force, were unemployed. In most cities, unemployed workers stood in "bread lines" to get free food from the government to keep themselves and their children from starving.[4]

More Supply Than Demand

Still, on the farm, Americans were not feeling depressed at all. If anything, they were more optimistic than ever. They were about to bring in their biggest crop on record. By this time, however, the European countries that had depended on the United States for food during World War I were now back to producing food for themselves. Farmers knew this would mean a drop in prices. So, in order to make a profit, they tried to break the law. It was not a federal, state, or local law they broke. It was a law of economics: the law of supply and demand.

To make up for the low prices they expected that year, farmers planted and harvested more wheat than ever before. Their efforts, combined with good weather, brought them a yield of 17.7 bushels per acre. Because of this huge harvest, supplies of wheat were far greater than the demand that year. Prices dropped to a

Law of Supply and Demand

The **price** of a product is determined by the difference between the **supply** (available quantity) and the **demand** (consumer need) for the product:

- When the supply is *greater than* the demand, prices are low.
- When the supply is *less than* the demand, prices are high.
- When the supply is *equal to* the demand, prices are average.

low of only twenty-eight cents per bushel, far less than the cost of production. Some farmers could not sell their wheat at all. Others bought huge storage bins, hoping to store the grain until the prices went back up.[5] Although many farmers vowed not to plant so much the next year, they did not know that this would be the last big crop they would see in many years.

The Dry Years Begin

By the time that harvest was finished in the spring of 1931, farmers had more than low prices to worry about. By early summer, rain was overdue. As usual, farmers plowed and planted in the fall, believing that rain would have to come soon. That winter, however, did not bring the usual rain and snow that farmers needed. As spring approached, it was clear that the winter wheat crop would be a failure, and most farmers did not even have money to buy seed to plant something else. A headline in the *Liberal News* on March 18, 1931, announced "Many Need Crop Loans." The farmers' desperate situation made them easy victims of con men who offered false loans to farmers. They promised lower interest rates than the farmers were currently paying on their mortgages. The swindlers collected fees for the application and processing of the loan, then disappeared with the farmers' money.[6]

Keeping Their Hopes Up

By May, many areas were too dry to have a good crop of wheat growing. According to Mr. W. V. Griffith of

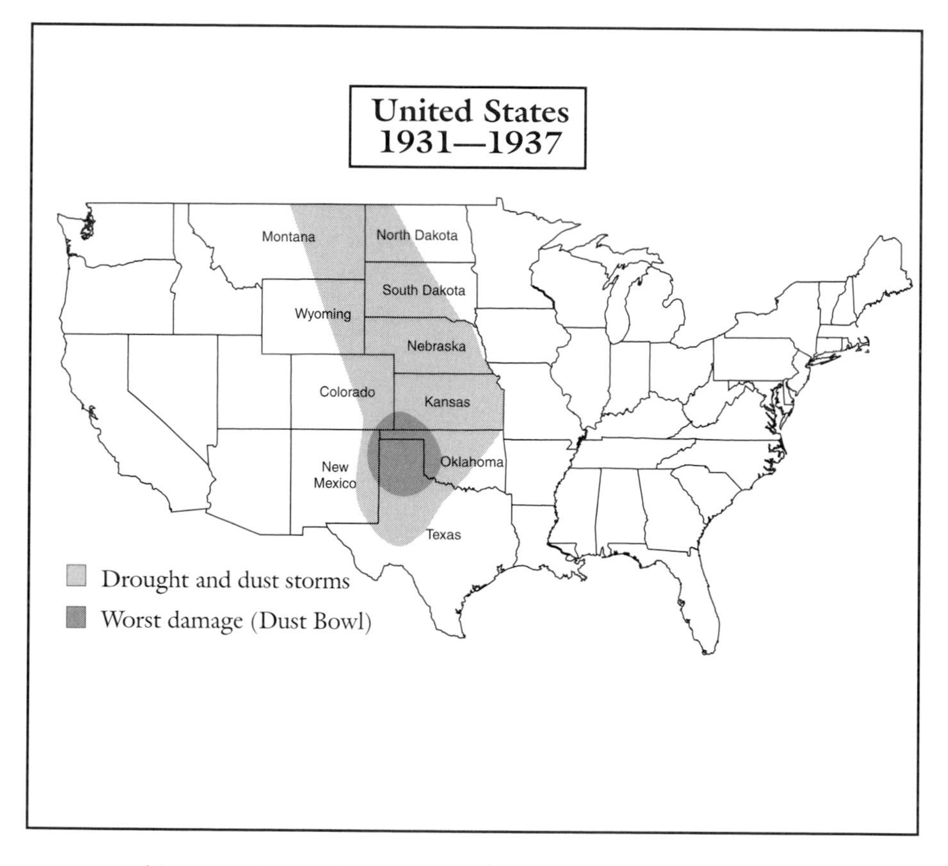

This map shows the parts of the United States affected by drought and dust storms.

Liberal, Kansas, most of the wheat in the area was "very spotted and generally poor" and was "badly affected by the dry weather." However, Griffith added, the farmers had not given up. They were now replanting the fields with row crops such as corn and sorghum (a grain plant similar to corn used for stock feed), confident that rain would come soon. He also noticed that more farmers had gone back to using horses to help with the farming instead of expensive gasoline-powered machinery.[7]

Farmers Important to the Economy

The difficult times for the farmers affected nearly everyone in the towns on the Plains. Local storeowners depended on the farm families to keep their business going. Banks, which were already struggling to stay in business, needed the farmers' loan payments. The John Deere Company, one of several large manufacturers of farm equipment, had given United States and Canadian farmers over $12 million in credit, which had not been repaid in 1932.[8] As times got worse, many farmers were not able to pay even their property taxes. In April 1932, the school district in Liberal, Kansas, cut teachers' salaries 15 to 22.5 percent because of the lack of money from taxes.[9]

Without money coming in from their crops, farmers tried to find other work. Unfortunately, many other people were trying to do the same. George Casey was a teenager in Hominy, Oklahoma, in the early 1930s. He made money by delivering newspapers, and his mother took in laundry to make a little extra income. "We were luckier than some," he recalled. "We had a garden, chickens, and a cow. We didn't miss any meals."[10]

Sprouting Cows

While farm families struggled to feed their children, they also had to figure out how to feed their animals. They had no crops to feed the livestock, no money to buy feed for them, and no grass growing for the animals to graze on. Ann Marie Low grew up in South Dakota and helped out on her family's farm. In her diary, dated June 30, 1931, she says, "Cattle are starving all over the state, and there is no market for them. Horses drop dead in the fields from the heat. The milk cows have so little to eat they are going dry. . . . If good rains don't come soon, the Big Pasture will last only until August. Then the cattle must go to market or starve."[11]

In fact, the only thing that was growing well was the Russian thistle, more commonly known as tumbleweed. The plants were a nuisance to farmers. When they dried and broke free from their roots, they would blow across the fields and get tangled on the barbed wire. The farmers found, though, that if they cut the tumbleweed when it was still green, the plants made fairly good food for cattle.

Claudene Davis was a teenager in Syracuse, Kansas, during this time. Her family farmed and also raised cattle. One of her funniest memories of the Dust Bowl era was the "sprouting cows." "Dad would put up stacks of Russian thistles for feed," she remembers.

"Eating into these stacks, the cattle would get thistle seeds mixed in with the dirt and matted hair on their backs. Later, when it did shower some, their flat hip bones sprouted!"[12]

Hard Times Get Even Harder

By 1933, the farmers of the Southern Plains were suffering more and more. Now three years into the

The Great Depression forced many Americans to depend on "bread lines" run by local charities. These lines helped feed many people who did not have jobs or money for food.

drought and the Depression, most were completely without money and resources. They had to depend on the local grocery store owner to let them have food on credit without knowing how the debt would be repaid. Ruth Townsend helped her husband's family run their grocery store in Phillips, Kansas. "I know we never were paid for some of the food people bought on credit. They intended to pay us, but it was a hard time for everyone. They had to feed their families. It was a time when neighbors helped each other."[13]

"Debts would increase yearly and hang over everyone," said Claudene Davis. Despite the hardships, families and communities stuck together. "We didn't feel too bad, wearing patched and darned clothing, having just a slice of bread and butter for a lunch," recalled Claudene. "We were all in the same pot!"[14]

Jean Gregg, who lived in Lawton, Oklahoma, also remembers her childhood as a happy one, despite the hard times. "Everybody was in the same fix, so we didn't know we were poor. Neighbors helped each other by sharing vegetables from their gardens."[15] Like Jean and her neighbors, most people tried hard to maintain a positive outlook. They held out hope that next week, next month, next year, the rain would return and the situation would be better. The next year, however, made it harder to keep that hope. That was when the dust really started to blow.

LIVING WITH THE DUST

Spring is always a windy season on the Southern Plains. The months of February, March, and April are known as "blow months" because of the strong winds that sweep across the prairie. As the wind kicked up in 1932, it took hold of the loose, sandy soil, which was no longer held in place by the native grasses that had been stripped from the surface of the land. Because of the drought, there was not enough growth of wheat or other crop to hold the soil, either.

A dust storm approaching across the prairie was a frightening sight. Like the one on Black Sunday, a typical storm would block out the sun and decrease visibility to a few feet or even less. Because of the way the storms would roll up on the horizon, they became known as "black rollers" or "dusters."

As the storms progressed, some of the residents claimed they could tell where the storm had started by the color of the dirt in it: red from Oklahoma, brown from Kansas, or yellow from Texas or New Mexico. Margaret Bourke-White was a photographer who worked for an airplane company. When her crew was grounded by the lack of visibility, she observed and photographed a storm as it approached:

> The storm comes up in a terrifying way. Yellow clouds roll. The wind blows such a gale that it is all my helper can do to hold my camera to the ground. The sand whips into my lens. I repeatedly wipe it away trying to snatch an exposure before it becomes completely coated again. The light becomes yellower, the wind colder. Soon there is no photographic light, and we hurry for shelter to the nearest farmhouse.[1]

A dust storm might last for a few hours, or even a few days. A dust storm that began on March 13, 1935, blew continuously over southeast Colorado and western Kansas for twelve days. In 1932, the residents of some areas of the Great Plains endured fifty-eight days of dust storms spread out at intervals through the year—a total equal to almost two months' worth of "dusty days." By 1935, that number increased to 102 days. By the end of the 1930s, the areas worst hit by the blowing dust had suffered through a total of 724 days of dust during the ten years.[2] That was enough to equal nearly two years of dust. It is no wonder that this decade has been called "The Dirty Thirties."

Lost in Dust

A person caught out in a dust storm could easily lose all sense of direction and become confused. Mrs. H. E. Keith of Dodge City, Kansas, was only a block from her house when a dust storm came in. She tried to run home, but the storm came too fast. Luckily, her husband knew she was near and stood in the doorway shouting to her so she could find the house. "I looked pretty dirty when I got in," she said, "but he seemed glad to see me."[3]

Not everyone was as lucky as Mrs. Keith. August Nelson, an elderly man who lived near Salina, Kansas, was found dead on his farm. The coroner's jury determined that he had been caught outdoors in his pasture when a dust storm swept through. Unable to find his way back, he had been suffocated by the dust.[4]

Claudene Davis and her siblings grew up riding horses on their farm near Syracuse, Kansas. When the dust storms began, they learned the practical way to get home. Her dad told them, "Let your horse go the direction it wishes. It will get you home." She found out this was good advice. "Many a time I have felt the horse was going wrong, but no, they have an inborn sense of direction."[5]

George Casey spent summers with a friend who lived on a ranch near Hominy, Oklahoma. One day while riding horses they saw a duster approaching. "We could see the house and barn, and behind that was a dust cloud coming. Even though we wanted to run the other way, we rode into the storm toward the fence. We were able to follow that fence back to the house, even though we couldn't see anything."[6]

Peril on the Road

Traveling by automobile was risky during the blow months. A motorist caught in a black blizzard would be instantly blinded by the blowing dirt. If he attempted to continue driving, he could end up crashing into something or running off the road. More likely, though, his car would stop running when the carburetor became choked with dust or static electricity caused the ignition to short out. Once stranded, he faced a difficult choice: stay in the car until the storm passed (which might be hours or even days), or go for help on foot through the blowing dust.

Margaret Davis and her sister Ruth were schoolteachers in rural Kansas in 1935. On March 17, 1935, they were driving home from school when they saw the sky to the north of them turn to dusty black. As the black storm hit, their car engine shorted out and stalled, leaving them stranded on the country road. "We huddled together to resist the cold March wind," Margaret recalls. "We did our best to keep warm until the wind lessened, then we started walking. We went about six miles before reaching a dwelling. The dear woman gave us her warm bed. As morning dawned the wind diminished, and the good ol' Kansas sun was shining."[7]

A Housekeeping Nightmare

Things did not improve much after a dust storm had passed. By the 1930s, most of the soddies had been replaced by houses made of wood or of dried bricks. Wooden houses often had gaps between the boards. Bricks would crumble in the dry weather and develop cracks. It was nearly impossible to keep out the dust that blew. Sometimes it became almost as dark indoors during a storm as it was outdoors, even with the lamps lit.

Homeowners tried many techniques to keep out the dust. Some used masking tape around doors and windows to keep the wind out. Others nailed damp sheets over the windows to catch the blowing dirt. Claudene Davis remembers her mother stuffing old feather pillows in windows where a pane was broken out. Still, the powdery dust found its way in.

The morning after a dust storm, a family would wake to find their beds covered with dirt. The only clean area would be the part of the pillows where their heads had rested. Their bare feet would land in dust that felt like flour spilled on the floor. Few housewives had vacuum cleaners at that time, so their main weapon in the war on dirt was a broom. Claudene even recalls using a shovel to clean out the bathtub after a big dust storm.

Despite the housewife's best efforts, it was impossible to clean out all the dirt. During the blow months it was even more discouraging because she knew another storm would probably fill the house again in a day or two. In some cases, the heavy dust accumulated in attics and caused ceilings to collapse, spilling a thick layer of dirt all over the house.

Clifford R. Hope was a congressman from Garden City, Kansas, during the Dirty Thirties. He took his family to Washington, D.C., with him in the fall of each year and closed the house in Garden City as tightly as possible with weather stripping. When the

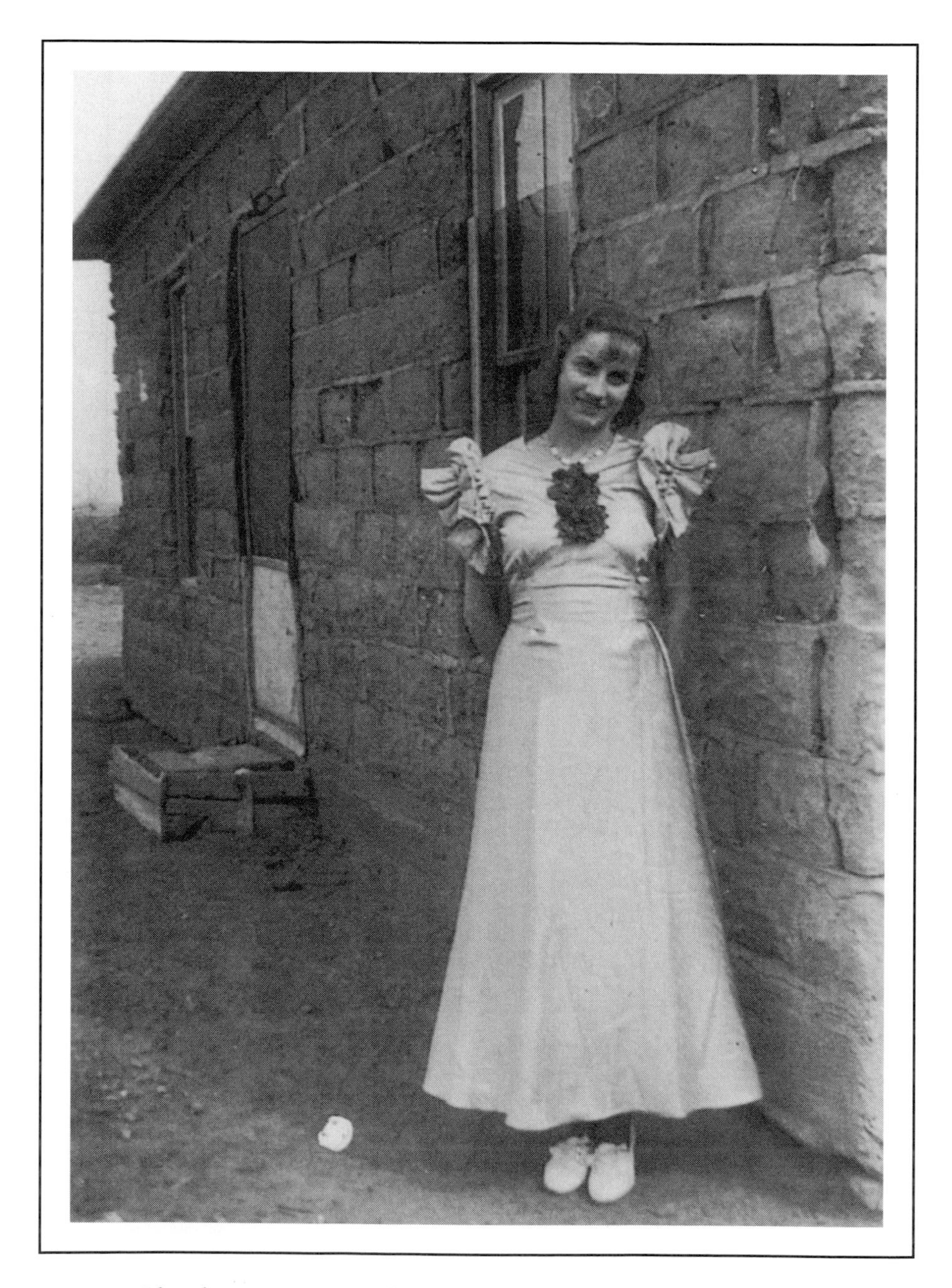

Claudene Davis stands next to her family's house. "Notice the cracks in the wall next to me," she writes. "It's no wonder we fought a constant battle with dust in the house."

family came back the next summer, they found a half-inch or more of dust covering everything. One year, sixteen truckloads of dirt had to be removed from the yard.[8]

Everything Tasted Like Dirt

Cooking and serving meals was one of the biggest challenges to the Dust Bowl residents. Dust fell into pans as food cooked on the stove. Some housewives used pressure cookers (pots with air-tight lids) to keep the dirt out. Washing food before cooking helped, but even that did not work for everything. When Claudene Davis and her brother Raymond would milk the cows, "we never made it out of the barn with anything but 'chocolate' [dusty-brown] milk."[9]

Even when cooked without dirt, food was often dusty by the time it was eaten. As they set the table for dinner, children turned the plates upside-down until the food was ready. The plates were turned upright when the food was served, but by the time dinner was over, they could write their names in the dust on the rims of the plates. In the typical fashion of Dust Bowl residents who tried to see the humor in any situation, Kansans referred to this element in their food as "Vitamin K," for the Kansas dirt.

Wash Day Blues

Since electric washers and dryers were not common (during this time many farms did not even have electricity), most farm wives washed clothes in tubs or pedal-operated washing machines. A hand-cranked device with rollers (called a wringer) would squeeze out most of the water from the clothes, which were then hung on a clothesline outdoors to dry. During the 1930s, clean-air days were few and far between. An unlucky housewife who had damp clothes on the line when a dust storm came up would find them caked with mud and needing to be washed again.

With water in short supply, even people did not get washed very often. A full bathtub was a luxury most people did not have. At Betty Riley's house in Johnson County, Kansas, their water came from a tank in the ground. "We could each have a teakettle of hot water for a bath, and we did not get that every day!" she said. She values water more today because of her experience. "I still cringe if I see people running water unnecessarily."[10]

Health Problems Caused by Dust

The constant dust in the air was more than just an inconvenience; it was also a danger to health. As the dust storms increased, more and more people had trouble breathing. Dust would choke their lungs and silica particles (a mineral in the dirt) would cause irritation and scarring of the lung tissue. A new disease called "dust pneumonia" was reported in all areas of the Dust Bowl. Young children and elderly people were most often affected, although many farmers who attempted to continue driving their tractors during dust storms also suffered from this illness.

In 1935, four hospitals in western Kansas reported that 17 percent of the patients they admitted in March suffered from acute breathing disorders. In April, the worst month for dust storms, 52 percent of patients admitted to those hospitals had breathing problems. With treatment, some were able to cough up large clods of dirt from their lungs. Others, about one patient out of every seven reported at these four hospitals, died of their illness.[11]

Deadly Measles

In the 1930s, there were no vaccinations to prevent measles. In most cases, a child with measles would be ill for a few days or a week, then return to school. In 1935, however, an epidemic of measles swept through the Dust Bowl region. It was far worse than usual and came at the worst time of the dust storms. That spring, thirty thousand people in southwestern Kansas suffered from measles, compared to eight thousand the year before.[12] Most of those were young children who were already suffering the effects of breathing in dust. Some of them were also weak from lack of good nourishment. Many children died of measles complicated by dust pneumonia.

Help From the Red Cross

It did not take long for people to realize that they could breathe better during a dust storm if they covered their faces with a cloth to filter the air they breathed. Some thought they got even better relief if the cloth was wet so that it trapped more dirt. Of course, in a really strong black roller, the dust would be so thick that the wet mask would soon be coated with mud and would need to be rinsed frequently. Also, since some storms lasted many hours, the constant breathing of moist air could further aggravate pneumonia.

In 1935, the American Red Cross began a campaign to make and distribute dust masks to residents of the Dust Bowl. Their design included several layers of cheesecloth (a loosely woven cotton fabric) sewn together, with strings to be tied around the head. Albert Evans, the national disaster relief director of the Red Cross, estimated that ten thousand masks were needed immediately for people who lived in the Dust Bowl areas of Kansas, Oklahoma, Texas, Colorado, and New Mexico.[13]

According to the Red Cross report, "Nine deaths within a week, 6,000 cases of measles and 200 'dust cases'—pneumonia aggravated by dust" required immediate action by the public. The health organization asked that "everyone wear masks in dust storms and cooperate with health officers in fighting disease."[14] A person traveling through the area for the first time and seeing everyone in masks might have thought he had arrived in the middle of a surgeon's convention or a bank robbery!

Healthy Dust?

Not everyone was convinced that the dust was bad for health, however. A story from the *Dodge City Daily*

The Red Cross urged all Dust Bowl residents to wear masks like these to help filter dust from the air they breathed.

Globe reported that many women were experiencing improved health due to the extra exercise of doing so much bending and sweeping to clean up the dust. Bill Shean of Spearville, Kansas, reported that his wife was "getting slimmer and feeling better than before." He was convinced that the work related to the dust actually made people feel better. One can only wonder if Mrs. Shean was as enthusiastic as her husband![15]

Dusty Communities

The Dirty Thirties required communities to make many adjustments to their normal routine. Some of the same problems that made more work for housewives made life harder for businesses, schools, churches, and other segments of society. Meetings were often cancelled because of dust storms, and the costs of cleaning up were hard on everyone.

Transportation at a Standstill

While blowing dust often caused cars to quit, there was another force at work: static electricity. As the gritty sand blew, it gathered an electrical charge. This electrical charge could short out a car's ignition and cause it to stall. When Margaret and Ruth Davis were stranded by a dust storm, they were surprised to see small flashes of light in the darkness outside their car. Margaret recalled, "Later we learned that the electricity of the wind hitting the barbed wire fence caused sparks from each barb on the wire."[1] Gas stations had to close during dust storms because of the danger of explosions caused by static.

Even after a black roller had passed, travel by automobile could be slow. A fierce storm would leave behind dunes of dust across roads. These would have to be cleared by road crews or by the people who lived on the road before cars could get through.

The same dust that halted traffic on the highways also built up on railroad tracks and blocked trains.

Scenes like this one in Amarillo, Texas, were common during the dust storms of the 1930s.

Giant drifts of dust would have to be cleared from the tracks. Sometimes trains waited days for tracks to be cleared by men with shovels, since even the snow plows used by the railroads could not remove the powdery dust from the rails. As a result, merchandise headed for or through the Dust Bowl was often delayed.

Unexpected Holidays

In most towns, students received some extra days of vacation because of the black blizzards. When the storms were most frequent, parents were afraid of children being caught in a dust storm as they walked to or from school. In Hays, Kansas, a little boy never made it home from school. His parents and neighbors searched for him for nearly twenty-four hours before they found him suffocated and nearly buried in dust.[2]

Most often, however, school schedules were altered to allow janitors more time to clean up after a storm. On March 18, 1935, the *Dodge City Daily Globe* reported that "Using scoop shovels, W. D. Orebaugh and his son Roy cleaned off the tables in the Center Star school Sunday, then unearthed the buried rugs and shoveled the dirt outside."[3] A month later, the city added twelve workers to its janitorial staff to help clean the schools and other public buildings.[4] The school day was even shortened by an hour to give the janitors more time to work.[5]

Businesses Buried in Dust

Although business was brisk in the sale of masking tape, brooms, and protective eye goggles, each dust storm was costly to local merchants. Besides the tasks of cleaning out their stores, they also had to bear the cost of merchandise ruined by the dust. Since most grocery stores protected their meats and baked goods in glass cases instead of the plastic wrap used now, most of these products would be ruined by dirt.

New clothing and hats in shops were often soiled beyond repair in department store windows. After one storm, the J.C. Penney department store in Dodge City, Kansas, displayed a sign in its front window announcing that the dust pile in the window represented a Nebraska farm that had just been blown in.[6]

Movies, Anyone?

The only business in town that seemed to be doing well during the storms was the local movie theater. Those who could afford the admission (usually five cents) enjoyed going to the movies. The theater in Dodge City advertised that its air-circulation system provided "water washed air." The manager reported that attendance was always good during a dust storm because audiences enjoyed the clean air in the theater. The day after a storm, however, attendance dropped to almost zero because people were busy cleaning up their homes.[7]

Disaster on the Farm

As if the drought were not hard enough on the farmers, the dust storms made life even more difficult. Expensive farm machinery could be quickly ruined by the blowing dust, which would clog the engine and deposit grit in the gears. A farmer who could not make the repairs himself faced expensive repair bills to keep his tractor running. In some cases, even new machinery was ruined by blowing dirt. A tractor on a dealer's

This orchard was destroyed by drifted dirt.

lot in Meade, Kansas, was ruined by dirt blown into the exhaust pipe as it sat for a week on display in the sales lot.[8]

The damage done to crops by the drought was also made worse by the blowing storms. Many farmers had the misfortune of seeing their seeds blown right out of the ground by the wind. Many did not have the money to buy more seeds to replace the lost crop.

Even when the plants stayed in the ground and received enough moisture to sprout they were not safe. Blowing soil from a neighbor's farm could bury an entire field in a single dust storm. A black blizzard would sometimes leave piles of dirt deep enough to cover the fence posts. Travis Gregg recalls that after a storm "a whole field would look like waves of white sand."[9]

Plants that survived these forces and somehow managed to form grain still faced another danger: The static electricity that shorted out car engines, disrupted telephone and radio communication, and created a light show on barbed wire fences could also burn wheat right on the stalk, ruining it.

Perhaps the worst hardship farmers faced was the damage to the land itself. In order to try to control blowing, farmers continued to plow the ground in different patterns. However, the additional plowing only broke up the dirt more, making it easier for the wind to pick it up. In severe blow areas, farmers lost feet of valuable topsoil from their farms. In some places, the fertile soil was all blown away, leaving only the hardened subsoil behind.

Claudene Davis and her brothers and sisters did not like the dust storms, but they did enjoy the "treasure hunts" they had afterward. The area near their home in Syracuse, Kansas, had once been home to several tribes of American Indians. After the wind had swept the top layer of dirt from the fields, the children would look for arrowheads. During the years of the dust storms, the Davises found dozens of arrowheads of all different sizes, ranging from small points less than two inches long to spearheads up to eight inches long.[10]

Dangers for Livestock

Besides losing their crops to dust, farmers also lost their livestock. When dust drifts formed along a fence, the dirt could build up as high as the top of the fence. Cattle would sometimes wander out of the pasture as they searched for food. Any vegetation they found to eat would be coated with the gritty soil left by the storms. After a while, the cattle died because their teeth wore down to the gums from chewing the sandy grit. Like people, cattle also suffered the effects of breathing and eating dirt. When a cow died for no apparent reason, the rancher might cut open its stomach to find a coating of dirt several inches thick.

Dust Bowl Pests

Cattle and people were not the only creatures going hungry during the drought. As vegetation and grass became more scarce, the countryside was invaded by hungry jackrabbits in search of food. They descended on the wheat fields, ready to destroy what little grain farmers had salvaged. Although the farmers were helpless to battle drought, blowing soil, and static electricity, this new enemy was something they were ready and willing to fight.

Throughout the Dust Bowl area, farmers organized "rabbit drives" to rid themselves of these pests. Armed with broomsticks, wagon wheel spokes, and golf clubs, men and boys herded the jackrabbits into fenced areas, where they clubbed the animals to death. Guns were banned from rabbit drives after the first attempts to use them resulted in more injuries to people than rabbits. In January 1935, over ten thousand rabbits "met their doom" in "the largest jackrabbit drive ever staged in western Kansas."[11] Although this may seem cruel, the rabbits were a very real threat to crops and to the survival of the people. According to Professor L. D. Wooster of Kansas State College, the jackrabbit population of western Kansas in March 1935 was estimated at 484 per square mile, more than triple the number in the same area just one year before.[12]

Besides lowering the rabbit population, the rabbit drives served some other important functions for Dust Bowl residents. Rabbits killed in the drives were usually given to families who needed food. Rabbit meat was a good source of nourishment for families who had little money and no livestock to provide meat. Rabbit drives also gave farmers a small feeling of control over the elements of nature that seemed to have turned against them. It was a way to relieve some of their frustrations and also help neighbors save their crops.

Another pest the Dust Bowl residents battled was harder to control: grasshoppers. These insects would arrive by the millions and invade the farmers' fields, destroying any crop they could find. Besides eating living vegetation in the fields, the grasshoppers would sometimes swarm into towns. They were known to eat even the paint off houses.

Humor Eases the Tension

The Great Plains farmer used humor to ease the suffering of the Dust Bowl years. Many jokes circulated about the severe drought. Like the tall tales of colonial America, the jokes started with reality and built their humor through exaggeration. Almost everyone heard about the farmer who was hit by a drop of rain and fainted from the shock. It took two buckets of sand thrown in his face to revive him.

Another popular joke told of a passing motorist who saw a hat on top of a dust dune by the side of the road. He stopped his car to investigate. When he lifted the hat, he was surprised to find there was someone under it. The motorist asked, "Do you need some help?"

"Naw." The man replied. "I'm on horseback."

Photographer Margaret Bourke-White heard a story about a pilot flying over Amarillo, Texas, whose plane stalled from the blowing dust. He jumped from the plane with his parachute, but it took him six hours to tunnel his way down to the ground.[13]

Even the animals of the Southern Plains were part of the tall tales. After a big dust storm, prairie dogs were said to be tunneling ten feet in the air. Crows, people said, flew backward to keep the dust out of their eyes.

Dust Bowl residents even made fun of themselves. Some questioned their own sanity in staying in this dusty area with stories like this one:

A traveler from California stopped at a gas station near Liberal, Kansas. "I don't know how you can stand this Dust Bowl," he told the gas station attendant. "Why, this country is nothing but a desert!"

"But, you have much worse desert in California," said the attendant.

"Yes, that is true enough," said the traveler, "but there aren't any fools out there trying to farm it!"[14]

Bad News

With the Great Depression affecting business and industry all over the country, little attention had turned to the farmers' troubles until the black blizzards became big news. As magazines, newspapers, and movie newsreels showed pictures of the dust storms, most Americans began thinking of the Southern Plains region as explorer Zebulon Pike had described it in 1806—a vast desert incapable of cultivation.

The bad publicity angered many Dust Bowl residents. Despite the current situation, most were loyal to

Shifting drifts of dust would soon force this farmer to abandon his home near Liberal, Kansas.

their own states and resolved to survive the drought and dust. Roy Bailey, editor of the *Salina Journal* in Kansas pointed out that the Plains farmers had endured hardships before. "We have come out of it before, and we will come out of it again," he said. ". . . [I]t has always called for courage, faith, loyalty, clear-thinking and honest effort. Those same elements are required today."[15]

6

Washington Lends a Hand

As the Depression gripped the nation in the early 1930s, President Herbert Hoover introduced measures intended to help banks and industry stay in business, but he did not begin any programs to provide relief directly to the poor and unemployed. Instead, he encouraged people to donate money to their local "community chests" (sometimes called the Poor Fund) to help their less fortunate neighbors.

In the cities, this type of fund could allow local groups to set up food pantries and other forms of aid to the poor. In the small rural towns of the Dust Bowl, however, nearly everyone was poor. Few people had enough money to pay their own bills, and they could not spare any to give away. Churches and other charitable organizations found themselves with less and less money with which to help more and more people.

Bankrupt Counties

When towns could not provide the money needed, they turned to the county government. Counties soon found themselves out of money to serve the poor. Most counties suffered from a lack of funds, since their money came from property taxes, and many people could not pay their taxes. States could not help much, either. They looked to the federal government in Washington, D.C., for help to take care of their poor.

Public campaigns urged people to donate clothing, bedding, and food to help their neighbors. President Hoover's Emergency Committee for Employment even urged those citizens who had jobs themselves to hire their neighbors to do work around the house such as painting, repairs, and cleaning. In this way, everyone could share the pride of working for a living. Welfare—money received from the government—was reserved for widows and those who were physically unable to work.

As the presidential election of 1932 approached, many farmers were angry at the lack of help President Hoover had given rural Americans. The president responded with the Emergency Relief and Construction Act (ERC), which set up a fund of $300 million to be given in loans to states to aid the needy. The ERC application process was complicated and confusing, however. By the end of 1932, less than 10 percent of the allotted money had been lent to the states.[1] Even though most farmers traditionally voted for the Republican candidate, they were now angry at Hoover and his party.

A New Deal

Most Americans felt it was time for a change, and Franklin Delano Roosevelt (FDR) promised just that—a New Deal for America. He charged that Hoover had been so busy looking out for the interests of business that he had ignored the common man. FDR pledged to commit himself to bettering the conditions of Americans. It would not be easy, though. Like most of its citizens, the federal government was also in debt. Roosevelt needed to balance the budget by controlling spending. He also had to provide relief for millions of Americans who were suffering in poverty.

Banks were still in deep trouble when FDR took office in March 1933. Worried Americans were crowding their local banks and withdrawing their money for fear that the bank would close as many others had. Just two days after his inauguration, FDR declared a national "bank holiday," requiring all banks to close for four days. This would give Congress time to draft a banking bill to improve the nation's economic

SOURCE DOCUMENT

I PLEDGE MYSELF TO A NEW DEAL FOR THE AMERICAN PEOPLE. LET US ALL HERE ASSEMBLED CONSTITUTE OURSELVES PROPHETS OF A NEW ORDER OF COMPETENCE AND OF COURAGE.[2]

Franklin Delano Roosevelt spoke these words on July 2, 1932, when he accepted the presidential nomination of the Democratic party.

health. Within a week, the panic that had gripped the nation began to ease.[3]

"Alphabet Soup" Helps Feed Americans

Next, FDR turned his attention to helping the millions of Americans who were poor and hungry. Over the next few years, he instituted so many plans and programs known by their initials that it was hard for people to keep up with them all. His critics sometimes referred to the many new programs as "alphabet soup," but President Roosevelt's programs were effective in providing needed relief to millions of Americans in all parts of the country, including the Dust Bowl.

Work for Young Men: The CCC

Legislators did not like the idea of giving money to people who were capable of work. Most citizens did not want to accept payments, either; they really wanted to work. With these ideas in mind, FDR introduced the Civilian Conservation Corps (CCC) during his first month in office.

The CCC employed young men whose families were on relief to work on conservation and reforestation projects. This program was operated by the War Department, and young men who joined the CCC were treated like soldiers. George Roberts of Higbee, Missouri, joined the CCC right after high school. He was stationed in a CCC camp near Fairfield, Iowa. "We lived in army barracks, with thirty men to each

This poster advertised the benefits of the CCC.

unit," he recalls. "We had to march and do other maneuvers." The CCC men were grateful to have three meals a day, free clothing, and medical care. George's brother Fay was stationed in Fayette, Missouri. He drove the ambulance for his CCC camp.[4]

The men were paid $30 a month, of which $25 was sent home to their families. Although that was not a large wage even at that time, it would be enough to help a young man's parents with some basic expenses. The CCC kept these young men busy with projects such as planting trees to block the wind and building lakes for recreation.

The CCC performed several important functions for the United States. It provided monetary relief for many families and gainful employment for young men who would otherwise be competing with older men for scarce jobs in the cities. It also benefited the public with its projects. In the seven years of its existence, the CCC employed over 2 million young men.

State-Administered Work: FERA

Just two months after the CCC began, Roosevelt introduced another program designed to provide relief for the poor. The Federal Emergency Relief Administration (FERA) provided money to states to be used to benefit the poor. The head of FERA, Harry Hopkins, directed states to administer work-relief programs. Men were hired to pave roads, build schools, and even to shovel dirt drifts from railroad tracks. Women were employed in sewing rooms to make clothing for themselves and other relief families, and to serve school lunches or help out on the school playground.

Wages for FERA jobs were low and could not really provide a decent standard of living for most families, but people involved in the program could receive government surplus food like rice, beans, and peanut butter. Most relief recipients did not like to depend on the government to feed and clothe their families, but they had no choice. James Dickenson's aunt, Opal Dickenson, recalled the clothing supplied by the relief sewing rooms: "The dresses all looked the same. A lot of women who got them would crochet lace or something as trim to put on the dresses to try to hide the fact that they were from the [government]."[5]

New Initials, Expanded Programs: CWA

In the fall of 1933, FERA was replaced by the Civil Works Administration (CWA). Although the initials were different, the idea was the same: to give people work so that they could earn money to support their families. Many of the same programs begun under FERA were continued, and new ones were added. Within two months, CWA was employing 4 million people to work on public projects such as building and repairing schools, airports, and highways.[6] CWA also gave jobs to people in more nontraditional fields, like artists and writers. This part of the program angered some people who wanted to see more useful products of work relief programs than words and pictures. After just a few months, CWA was discontinued and FERA was reinstated with new money.

Work for Students: NYA

In 1935, FDR established the National Youth Administration (NYA) to help give young people "their chance in school, their turn as apprentices, and their opportunity for jobs."[7] A fund of $50 million was set up to provide employment for high school and college students ages sixteen to twenty-five. High school students received $6 a month; college students were paid $15 a month. This aid was administered through the schools, according to each student's

Betty Klinger's NYA job teaching swimming classes at the YMCA helped her continue her college studies.

financial need. Most students worked in their schools in libraries and laboratories. Although the wages were low by today's standards, this program allowed many students to stay in school instead of dropping out to try to find jobs.

Bigger and Better: The WPA

In 1935, the largest work-relief program of the New Deal began. The Works Progress Administration (WPA) has been called "the biggest, most ambitious, and generally most successful relief program the federal government has ever undertaken."[8] Actually, FDR did not like to call the WPA a relief program. His idea was to employ people in useful work to serve the citizens of America, and to pay the workers a decent wage.

WPA projects included construction of highways, hospitals, schools, courthouses, airports, and other facilities to serve the public. Many of these projects, including Boulder (Hoover) Dam, are still in use today. One of the largest WPA projects was the Tennessee Valley Authority (TVA). For this project, WPA workers built dams to control erosion, prevent flooding, and produce electrical power for people living along the Tennessee River.

Over the course of the five years of its existence, the WPA employed an average of over 2 million people on each monthly payroll. By 1941, it had given jobs to over 8 million Americans, approximately 20 percent of the total workforce in the country. One important benefit of the program was that the money paid to workers

The Hiawassee Dam in North Carolina was built as part of the Tennessee Valley Authority, the largest project of the Works Project Administration (WPA).

was put back into the economy immediately, as the workers used it to buy goods and pay bills.

About one fifth of the money allocated for the WPA went to community service programs that employed people with various skills such as artists, historians, musicians, dentists, and others. FDR's reasoning was that all people had a right to work according to their own talents, even if they were not construction workers.

Of course, all government programs have critics, and the WPA was no exception. Some people joked that WPA workers were often seen leaning on their shovels instead of working, and that WPA stood for

"We're Probably Asleep." A musical comedy written and performed by WPA-employed performers responded to this criticism in a skit called "Leaning on a Shovel":

When you look at things today
Like Boulder Dam and TVA
And all those playgrounds where kids can play
We did it—by leaning on a shovel![9]

As with CWA, some people objected to paying federal money to artists, playwrights, and musicians. More serious was the charge that some WPA officials used their influence for corrupt political purposes, like pressuring workers to vote Democratic.

Work relief programs helped many Americans by giving them work and wages at a time when both jobs and money were scarce. Although these were programs for all states, Dust Bowl residents, whose main livelihood—farming—could no longer support them, found them vital to survival. Even though wages for work-relief programs were low, they allowed millions of people to work and retain their dignity through difficult times.

7

Washington Helps the Farmers

As FDR planned relief programs, he did not neglect the problems of American farmers. In May 1933, Congress passed the Agricultural Adjustment Act (AAA). One goal of the AAA was to improve the balance between supply and demand for farm products. The price crash of 1931 had been caused when farmers produced more crops than were needed. The AAA intended to reduce production in order to bring prices back up to a reasonable level. Farmers, however, still believed that the only way they could make a profit was to produce as much as possible. It would not be easy to convince them to deliberately produce less.

Getting Paid for Not Working

The AAA's solution was to pay farmers to keep part of their land out of production. Critics of the AAA said it was foolish to pay farmers for not working, but the goal of the plan was logical. If production decreased, prices would go up again and farmers could make a profit. Dust Bowl farmers had mixed reactions to it,

Severe soil erosion left many fields on farms all across America looking like this.

but most were glad to receive some aid, especially since the drought was making it so difficult to raise any wheat. For many Dust Bowl farmers, AAA payments were their only income.

The AAA plan paid farmers according to the average yield per acre in their own county. In Meade County, Kansas, for instance, the government calculated the average yield at 12.5 bushels of wheat per acre. To receive AAA payments, a farmer had to leave 15 percent of his acreage uncultivated. Calculated at a price of eighty-four cents per bushel, a farmer would receive about $10.50 from the AAA for each acre he did not farm.[1]

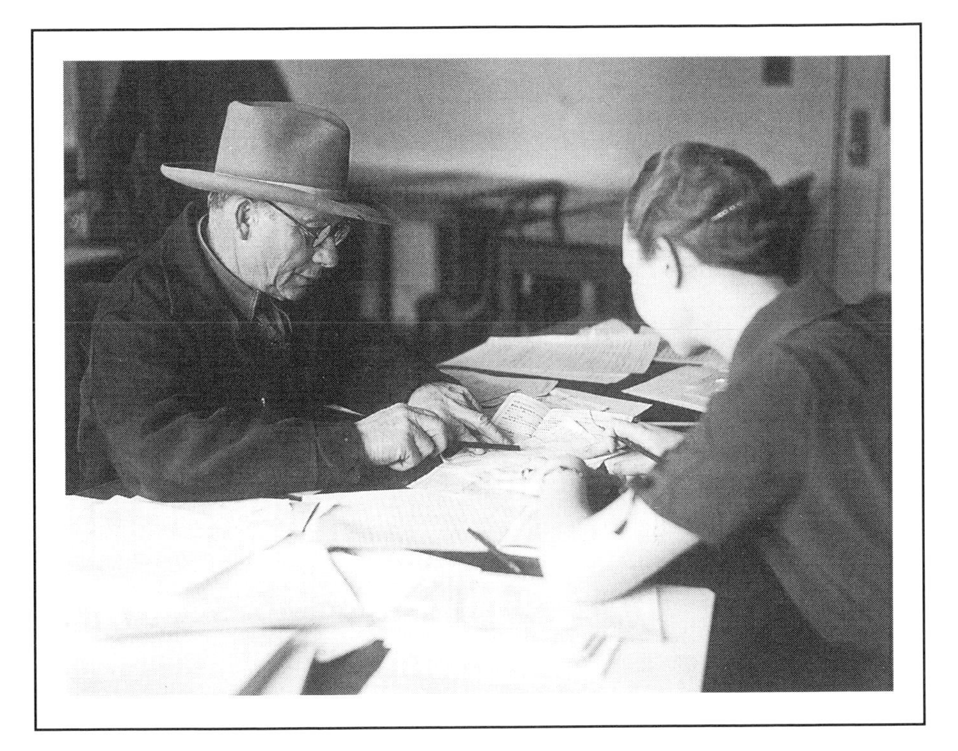

This farmer is signing a wind erosion agreement. He will receive government payments to control blowing soil on his land.

Like many Dust Bowl farmers, Lawrence Svobida went through the process of applying for AAA funds. He had just endured the loss of another wheat crop in May 1933 and was ready to accept any help the government would give. Some of his neighbors, however, were not so enthusiastic about the AAA. He said,

> There were mouthy individuals who seized every opportunity to run down this entire program, . . . condemning it as useless, crooked, revolutionary, or dictatorial; but it was noteworthy that when the first AAA payments were made available, shortly before

> Christmas, the same wordy critics made a beeline to the courthouse. They jostled and fell over each other in their mad scramble to be first in line to receive their allotment money.[2]

In addition to payments for reduced production, the AAA also helped farmers in other ways. The government bought some surplus goods that could not otherwise be sold, and it made loans to farmers who had no collateral (money or property) to secure the loan except their next crop.

AAA programs were financed by a tax paid by processors who used the farm products. For instance, a manufacturer of fabric would pay taxes on cotton purchased, and a flour mill would pay taxes on wheat. In this way, the producers (farmers) were able to make more profit.

Cattle Buyouts

Along with controlling production of plant crops, the AAA also made efforts to control farm animal overproduction. Beginning in June 1934, the AAA could purchase surplus pigs and beef cattle. In the Dust Bowl, the animals were near starvation because farmers could not grow enough food or afford to purchase feed for them. Most of the purchased animals were slaughtered. The meat was distributed to relief families. Animals too ill or weak to provide good meat were destroyed.

In Kansas alone, the AAA purchased over half a million head of beef cattle in 1934, at a total price of

The government purchased millions of starving cattle from farmers who could not afford to feed them. The animals were slaughtered and the meat given to poor families.

$7,523,349.[3] The program certainly benefited those who received the meat and helped farmers gain income from animals that may have been impossible to market.

The Farmer Speaks

One interesting feature of the AAA was that the renewal of the program that paid benefits to farmers had to be approved by the farmers themselves through a vote. In May 1935, when the program had its second anniversary and was due for renewal, the AAA director of the division of grains, George Farrell, made a visit to Dodge City, Kansas, to urge farmers to vote for continuing the AAA. "Remember that this matter of continuing the wheat program is one that rests entirely with the wheat farmer," he told them. "The decision the wheat farmers will make on May 25 will be based largely on how well you and your neighbors understand the true facts about wheat."[4] As expected, the farmers voted to continue the program.

Bad Publicity for the AAA

Although the AAA had worthy goals, some farmers did not like the methods it sometimes used to accomplish those goals. A neighbor of Lawrence Svobida

The Agricultural Adjustment Act (AAA) was part of the New Deal for America that Roosevelt (with glasses, second from right) had promised on the campaign trail.

made a mistake in calculating the amount of land he was supposed to withhold from cultivation in 1934. When informed that he had seeded eighty acres more than he was supposed to, the farmer asked to be allowed to harvest the extra wheat, then turn it over to the county to be given to the needy. The AAA official rejected his offer and ordered the wheat destroyed.[5] Rumors of food crops and cotton being plowed under during a time when many Americans were starving and wearing rags did not please farmers or legislators.

A group of four thousand farmers from twenty-five states paid a visit to Washington, D.C., in May 1935. Although it appeared to be a mob scene at first, it soon turned into a joyous rally when FDR came out to address the crowd. He denied rumors of wasted products, telling the farmers,

> It is high time for you and for me to carry, by education, knowledge of the fact that not a single program of the AAA contemplated the destruction of an acre of food crops in the United States in spite of what you may read or be told by people who have special axes to grind.[6]

Still, there are enough accounts to believe that incidents of destruction did occur, although they may have been carried out by county AAA officials who used their own, not federal, authority.

In general, the AAA did a great deal to help farmers all across the United States. In the first two years of its existence, it collected $777 million in taxes from processors, distributed $678 million in benefit payments to farmers, and spent $191 million purchasing surplus crops and cattle and hogs. During this time prices also rose, and the national total of farm income increased from $4 billion to over $6 billion, although some of that gain was due to price increases caused by drought and the devaluation of the dollar.[7]

In the Dust Bowl regions, federal aid allowed many families to stay on their farms. In southwestern Kansas, the population on farms during the 1930s decreased as people moved away. Still, the population decrease was only about half the rate of decrease that occurred during the 1889–1895 drought when no federal aid was available.

The AAA brought hardship to some farmers, especially tenant farmers—those who lived on and farmed land owned by others. Often, landlords used the AAA payments to buy equipment, which reduced the need for hired labor. The tenant farmer could then be fired and forced to move from the land.

AAA Repealed; SCDAA Introduced

The programs of the AAA continued to draw fire from Congress. Processors objected to paying taxes to finance the AAA. After a legal battle, the United States Supreme Court declared the AAA unconstitutional in 1936. Farmers who had been depending on AAA payments and had reduced cultivation of their land for that reason, worried that they would not receive the payment they expected that year. The House of

SOURCE DOCUMENT

NO CRACKED EARTH, NO BLISTERING SUN, NO BURNING WIND, NO GRASSHOPPERS ARE A PERMANENT MATCH FOR THE INDOMITABLE AMERICAN FARMERS.[8]

President Franklin Delano Roosevelt made these comments in his "Fireside Talk" radio broadcast on September 6, 1936.

Representatives and the Senate quickly passed the Soil Conservation and Domestic Allotment Act (SCDAA), which continued many of the programs, although with a slightly different goal: soil conservation.

The parts of the AAA that had troubled the Supreme Court were eliminated from the new SCDAA program. The government would now pay farmers for practicing soil conservation techniques. The program would be financed by taxpayer dollars instead of by processors' taxes. Some critics, however, believed the SCDAA was written only to satisfy the Supreme Court and did not demonstrate a real change in policy. They said it was still the AAA, but with "a thick layer of soil-conservation paint for Supreme Court inspection."[9] Two years later, a revised AAA was made into law.

Power to the Farm People: REA

Although not a relief program, the Rural Electrification Act (REA) was important for millions of rural residents. The REA provided money to build and operate power plants and install power lines so that farm families could have electricity in their homes.

Until this time only about 10 percent of rural homes had electricity. Most city dwellers by now were using electric lights, refrigerators, and washing machines. Thanks to the REA, farm families could now have the opportunity to have these conveniences. Farm life could be made easier by the use of electric milking machines and other equipment. This legislation improved the living conditions and lightened the workload of millions of Americans.

Cutting Losses: The RA

One reform measure that was a blessing for some but drew much criticism was the Resettlement Administration (RA). By 1935, it seemed that perhaps explorer Zebulon Pike had been right: Some of the land in the Southern Plains was not suitable for farming. The farmers who owned this property had been able to raise crops only in years of higher-than-normal rainfall, such as the 1920s. Now, with drought conditions, some of them wanted to move away but were unable to sell their land. The RA's plan was to buy this "submarginal" land, return it to grassland, and resettle the farmers on better land elsewhere. In this way, farmers could be self-sufficient and would not need to rely on government relief money. For farmers who were tired of the dust and discouraged by the drought, it was just the opportunity they needed to get out of the Dust Bowl.

During its years of operation, the RA bought about 9 million acres of land and settled families in other areas of the country. Some farmers were sent to "model communities" built by the RA in various locations around the country. Others were simply paid for their land and given some money for moving expenses. In 1937, the RA was reorganized and renamed the Farm Security Administration (FSA). It continued purchasing land until 1947.

Many people resented the government's efforts to force them to give up their land. They did not want Washington lawmakers or FSA officials telling them what was best for their families. Many complained that FSA agents pressured farmers to sell good farmland.

Ann Marie Low's father was pressured by a government agent who wanted to purchase the family's land for a planned wildlife refuge. Some neighbors had already sold their land for a fraction of the money they had paid for it. Others, who were in debt to a bank, lost their land when the bank sold it to the RA. Ann Marie's father did not want to sell, but he knew that if he refused, the government could declare the land condemned and take it.[10]

The RA program also caused problems for some counties. Counties that had once had a thriving population of landowners who had paid taxes to support the county, now had large areas with almost no population. The land, which had once been taxable property, was now owned by the government. The loss of property tax income made it harder for counties to run schools and provide other services.

While some government programs were more successful than others, overall they provided needed aid to many people. There is no doubt that without the government relief offered to farmers, many more people would have been forced to leave their land. Still, many people could not survive, even with government help. As the dusty conditions worsened, many farmers took their families and went in search of a better life outside the Dust Bowl.

The Great Migration

When the dust storms first began, people remained optimistic. Robert Geiger, a reporter for the Associated Press, visited farmers in the Oklahoma panhandle, one of the areas hit hardest by the drought in 1935. He spoke with more than one hundred farmers, and not even one of them intended to leave the area. They all expected rain to come soon and planned on harvesting a crop that year.[1]

Taking to the Road

As the dust storms became more frequent, more Dust Bowl residents decided to leave. The first to go were the tenant farmers. Since they farmed land owned by others, they often did not receive any benefit from the government aid offered through the AAA. They also had little at stake, since they had no money invested in the land. They could take their knowledge of farming and find work elsewhere. In 1935, families like those described by Margaret Bourke-White had become a frequent sight on the roads:

> We passed them on the road, all their household goods piled on wagons, one lucky family on a truck.

> All they owned in the world was packed on it; the children sat on a pile of bureaus topped with mattresses, and the sides of the truck were strapped up with bed springs.[2]

As conditions worsened, many landowners also left. If they had been on the Plains only a few years before the drought began, they had probably lost more crops than they had harvested. At this point, the land had become worthless; they could not sell it at any price. Some farmers who still had a mortgage on their property let the bank take it back. The Resettlement Administration (RA) helped others by buying their land and moving them to better land in other parts of the country. When the RA took

A migrant family on the road.

population statistics in forty counties in the Dust Bowl, it found that from 1935 to 1937, over a third of the farm population had left the region.[3]

Exodusters and Okies

Poverty and crop loss were only part of the reason why so many left the Southern Plains. Many people found the frequent dust storms unbearable. Parents feared for their own health and that of their children. Besides the dangers of the dust, the unending work of trying to clear the drifts of dirt from the barn, machinery, and house was just too much for many people. Long days and even weeks of dust without seeing the sun were hard on the spirit. Sometimes the farmers were so glad to get away from the farms they were leaving behind that they did not even bother to shut the door of the house behind them.

These wanderers became known as "exodusters" as they fled their dusty homeland, much like the followers of Moses did in the book of Exodus in the Bible. The Oklahoma panhandle was one of the worst areas for dust storms. As thousands of Oklahoma refugees made their way across the country to seek opportunity, they became known as "Okies." Eventually, this term came to identify all the Dust Bowl migrants, no matter where they had come from.

Some of the migrants left their farms intending to come back when the rains came again. Many of them took their families to neighboring states or counties outside the Dust Bowl to stay for a while with relatives.

Some Okies camped in California while they looked for work at local farms.

Others went farther west to look for work on the big corporate farms in California.

Help Wanted in California

Large food companies that harvested fruits and vegetables for canning and delivery to grocery stores operated many of the farms in California. They grew many crops such as peaches, oranges, peas, and lettuce. They needed thousands of workers to help pick the crops, but only for a limited period of time when each crop became ripe. Jobs would last for several weeks, then workers would move on to another farm to harvest a different crop. Growers needed the help, because new immigration laws had cut off the flow of Mexican laborers who had worked for low pay. Pay and working conditions were very poor for the farm workers, but since there were two or three migrants competing for every farm job, they could not demand better pay or conditions.

The migrant farm workers received a poor reception in California. Most arrived with no money, and many camped alongside the road in their cars. Those who could not find farm work went into the cities and applied for federal relief. In November 1935, a new federal regulation denied aid to these transients. In February 1936, city officials and the chief of police of Los Angeles sent policemen to patrol the borders of the state and turn away people who arrived with no money and no job. In the first four days, police turned away over a thousand people and jailed those who refused to turn back.[4]

Steinbeck and the Okies

John Steinbeck was one of several writers of the period who brought the plight of these refugees to the attention of the American public. His book *The Grapes of Wrath* told of the hardships of the Joad family from Oklahoma. Although the book offended many people because of the language and scenes it portrayed, it became a best-seller. It made people all across the country sympathize with the Okies and their troubles.

Eventually, the FSA recognized the need for decent housing for migrant farm workers. It constructed and managed many migratory labor camps in California. The camps provided temporary housing for migrant workers. In these camps, the government provided medical personnel and schools for the workers and their families. Although the living conditions were not luxurious, the camps did allow the workers a better home for their families than living out of their cars.

The Last American Frontier

One program sponsored by FERA provided an ambitious plan to help remove farmers from submarginal land and resettle them on better land. About two hundred families who were receiving government relief were chosen to become part of an experimental community in the Matanuska Valley in Alaska. At this time, the population of the Alaska territory was increasing as more workers moved there because of the growing mining industries. Food for the workers had to be imported because, even though there was good land for farming, there was no one to farm it. The families chosen for this project received farms in the Matanuska Valley for a small cost, which could be repaid over a period of ten years.

The families who took part in the experimental colony were chosen from depressed farming areas of Minnesota, Wisconsin, and Michigan. Some, like the Clyde Cook family who had moved to Minnesota from Stillwater, Oklahoma, were Dust Bowl refugees.[5] With twenty hours of daylight each day during the

During the Dust Bowl, many mothers of farming families wondered how long they would be able to provide for their children. This famous photo was taken by Dorothea Lange.

growing season, the farmers of the new town, Palmer, Alaska, were able to produce vegetables of record size.

The project was not a complete success, however. Settlers complained of poor living conditions and broken promises from government officials. Some resented the many rules forced upon them; others could not stand the swarms of mosquitoes that invaded the territory. Within a few years, many of the families had left Palmer. Some of the pioneers stayed, however, and their descendants still live there today.[6]

Many Left; More Stayed

Although many people left the Dust Bowl region during the 1930s, many more stayed. A visitor to this area would see many abandoned farms, and might conclude that the area was deserted, but that would be far from the truth. Overall, about one fourth of the population of the entire Dust Bowl area left. As the RA found in its study, the proportion of farm residents who moved away was higher—about one third. Still, that means that the majority of people stayed in the area. Claudene Davis's family never seriously considered leaving, even in the worst of times. "We had no money to go anyplace," she said. "We had nothing but the land, and you couldn't give it away."[7] For those who stayed, it was clear that they would have to change their methods of farming in order to stop the blowing dirt and preserve the topsoil.

9 WORKING WITH NATURE

The daily battle with dust was hard, but farmers had a more serious problem to worry about: the loss of their livelihood as their topsoil blew away. The farmer and his family could clean the dust out of the house, but they could not replace the valuable soil once it blew past the fence. Many farmers watched helplessly as the wind blew their soil away, leaving only the hardpan—the concrete-hard surface that lay beneath the topsoil.

In other parts of the country, serious flooding was washing soil from fields into the rivers. By 1934, soil erosion was a serious problem, and it was clear that overfarming was to blame. "I brought the first tractor to this county," said Judge Noel McDade, a farmer from the Texas panhandle. "I often think that somebody ought to have met me at the line and turned me back. I wouldn't ask for anything if my land were back in grass."[1]

Taming the Dust Bowl: The SCS

By April 1935, most of the country was just beginning to learn of the problems of the Dust Bowl. Since 1933,

Hugh Hammond Bennett was director of the Soil Erosion Service and the Soil Conservation Service during the Dust Bowl.

however, the Soil Erosion Service (SES), under the leadership of Hugh Bennett, had been monitoring soil conditions and advising farmers to make changes in their methods in order to preserve the soil. He believed that more than 50 million acres of American farmland had already been destroyed, and that another 100 million acres had lost almost all their productive topsoil.[2] He recommended new farming methods for the Great Plains, but they were not widely practiced.

The SES was intended to be only a temporary program. Bennett believed that the problem of soil erosion was serious, and he was frustrated that farmers and legislators did not seem to be concerned about it. On the day he went to Congress to ask its support, he heard that a heavy duster out of New Mexico was headed for Washington, D.C. He stalled the proceedings until a heavy yellow haze descended on the nation's capital. As darkness fell in midday, he addressed the legislators, saying, "This, gentlemen, is

SOURCE DOCUMENT

IF A FOREIGN NATION SHOULD INVADE THE COUNTRY AND DYNAMITE TO A STATE OF DESOLATION 35,000,000 ACRES OF THE LAND...WE PROBABLY WOULD BE HIGHLY INCENSED OVER SUCH TRESPASSING. THAT A PROCESS OF NATURE HAS BEEN THE GUILTY PARTY, . . . FOR SOME STRANGE REASON STRIKES US AS NOTHING TO BE ALARMED ABOUT.[3]

Hugh Bennett, director of the SCS, made this statement before a subcommittee of the House of Representatives Committee on Public Lands on March 20, 1935.

what I have been talking about."[4] On April 27, 1935, Congress established the Soil Conservation Service (SCS) as part of the United States Department of Agriculture (USDA), and made Hugh Bennett its director.

Getting Farmers to Cooperate

Bennett had many ideas to help farmers keep their land from blowing away. Not all the farmers were eager to adopt these new methods. Some resented the interference of the government in their business. Others objected that the measures suggested by Bennett would be expensive and time-consuming, not to mention a lot of work. Most of them were still hoping that rain would come soon and the problem would take care of itself. Under the old AAA, the goal had been to reduce production of farm products in order to stabilize prices. In the Dust Bowl region, nature had already drastically reduced production. Now the problem was that the nation's richest farmland was in danger of becoming completely barren. The SCS had to show farmers how to save their land and also provide financial support for their cooperation.

Listing the Soil

The first method of conserving the soil was one that many farmers were already aware of, but few practiced: listing. To list his fields, a farmer would use a plow with a deep double blade to cut furrows into the field. He would plow the furrows in a direction perpendicular to the direction the wind usually blew. If the winds usually blew from the north or south, for

A farmer lists his fields under the wind erosion program.

instance, the farmer would plow the furrows in an east-west direction. The plowing would bring the firmer dirt to the surface and cover over the drier, looser soil. When the wind blew, it would blow toward the sides of the plowed furrows, which would catch the blowing dirt. Federal money provided gas and oil to help farmers run their tractors to list their fields. Farmers who used horses to pull the listing plow received feed for their animals.

Listing the soil was only partially effective. Once the wind blew soil into the furrows, the listing had to be done again. The frequency of dust storms meant that farmers were often out in their fields trying to get the listing done during dust storms. Another problem with this method was the plowing itself, which caused the soil to become more and more powdery with every plowing. This made it blow even more.

Probably the biggest frustration, however, was for farmers who listed their land while their neighbors did not. No matter how hard a farmer worked to keep his own land from blowing, it did not help much if the next farmer allowed his soil to blow. A growing crop could be smothered in a day by soil blowing in from the next farm. Lawrence Svobida grew frustrated with his neighbors, "who simply did not feel like making the effort to check their land from blowing. They felt that losing a crop was tough enough, without battling the wind."[5]

Contour Farming

Another method intended to help stop both wind and water erosion of soil was contour farming. This technique was more work than just listing fields. It was used in areas where the ground was on a slope. Deep furrows plowed across the sides of hills would catch and hold rain and snow better than rows plowed up and down hills.

An experimental farm in Goodwell, Oklahoma, showed the effectiveness of contour farming. Two plots of land in the same field were compared. One was listed in straight lines up and down the slope; the other

Contour plowing, with furrows curved around the sides of a slope instead of straight up and down the slope, helped reduce both water and wind erosion by better retaining moisture.

was plowed in contours around the side of the slope. A brief but heavy rain shower of .08 inches fell on both fields. On the straight-plowed land, the rain soaked in to a depth of 8.12 inches. On the contour-plowed field, the rain soaked to a depth of 18.06 inches.[6]

Soil conservation was not limited to the Dust Bowl. While nearly 70 percent of the nation was suffering from drought, other areas had too much rain, causing soil to wash away. Contour farming helped both situations. In most cases, ordinary tractors could not make the contours needed. Since the job required more labor and heavier equipment than most farmers had, this became a project for the CCC. George Roberts of Higbee, Missouri, helped make contours on farms near Fairfield, Iowa. "They moved some of the dirt with big equipment," he said, "but we worked mostly with shovels and plows to make the contours."[7]

Strip Farming

Another method to keep soil from blowing was strip farming. Farmers would plant their wheat crop in long strips on their fields with a different crop planted in strips between the rows of wheat. In some areas, sorghum was planted on the alternate strips. In other areas, the alternate crop might be corn or even grass. Of course, this made the planting and harvesting processes a little more complicated, but conservationists reasoned that if the wheat failed, at least the other plants could help hold the soil in place. It was hard for farmers to give up part of their fields for a low-cash crop, but SCS payments helped. They also hoped that once the drought broke, they would be able to make money from wheat again if they could just keep their soil.

Shelterbelts

The CCC provided the manpower for another big project to stop blowing soil: planting shelterbelts of trees. President Roosevelt became the driving force behind this idea, although Congress at first did not want to fund the project. Since everyone knew that trees could block the wind and provide relief from heat, it seemed only logical that rows of trees, planted alongside fields, could help block the wind and control wind erosion. Experts who studied the climate, however, argued that planting trees in the Dust Bowl region was useless: the dry, hot climate would kill them.

Eventually, Roosevelt won the battle, and 220 million trees were planted by the CCC. The trees did little to help the Dust Bowl, however, since they were planted in rows just to the east of the 100th meridian, in the area judged to be more suitable for them. The shelterbelt zone is a long zigzag line extending from the middle of North Dakota's border with Canada down through Abilene, Texas. The trees survive to this day and have served to block the wind coming east from the Great Plains.

Irrigation

Irrigation—providing water artificially to dry farmland—is a common farming practice today. In the 1930s, however, it was a science that was only just beginning to catch on in the Dust Bowl. Irrigating with groundwater (water from streams and rivers) had been practiced for many years, but there was not enough groundwater in the Dust Bowl for farmers to use. Fortunately, another source of water was right under their feet. By the end of the 1930s, the Ogallala Aquifer, a huge table of water below the surface of the Great Plains, had been discovered. A deep well, with the aid of a windmill, could bring up the water needed to make the land productive again. Getting the water from the well to the fields was a challenge, however. It was an expensive process and many farmers could not afford the equipment and materials needed for irrigation.

Back to Grass

One of the more radical but most effective means of soil conservation did not involve farming at all. It was the end of farming in areas that the USDA determined should never have been farmed in the first place. Once the RA (and later the FSA) had purchased land from farmers, the next job was to return that land to its natural state.

In 1938, the SCS took over the management of the federally owned lands. It took years of reseeding and cultivation to bring the land back to its former state. In 1960, the lands were reopened as the National Grasslands. They are now managed by the United States Forest Service and include twenty different grasslands sites. Seven of these sites are in the former Dust Bowl areas of Colorado, Kansas, Texas, Oklahoma, and New Mexico.[8] Although these areas were once considered a wasteland, they are now full of wildlife and provide recreational opportunities such as camping, hiking, and fishing.

Blowing Soil Controlled

By 1937, the conservation measures of the SCS had begun to slow wind erosion. Even though the drought continued, blowing soil had decreased by about 60 percent. Without the constant battle against dust, life became more tolerable. Still, the problems of poverty and hunger persisted. Irrigation offered hope for agriculture, but rain—the one element that would guarantee survival—still did not come.

Slow Recovery

Plains farmers need at least eighteen inches of rain a year in order to grow wheat. In the years of the Dust Bowl, the average rainfall was only about fifteen inches a year, with some years having as little as eleven inches.[9] The winter of 1937–1938 brought more moisture than the previous years, so farmers were hopeful that a good crop would follow. Newspaper headlines announced that 1938 would see the biggest harvest in years, despite late freezes, hailstorms, and a harvest delayed by rain. "Soon the adversities of the past will be lost in rapidly dimming memory," wrote an optimistic newspaper reporter.[10] When the final count was

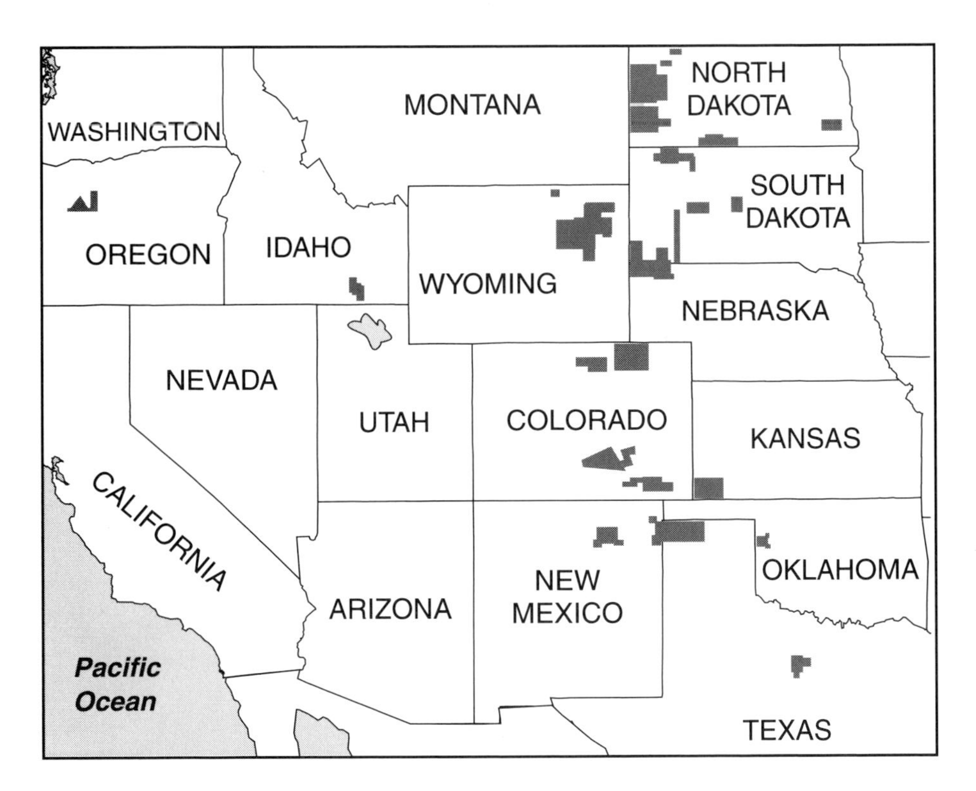

The National Grasslands (indicated by shaded portions) still exist today in many western and midwestern states.

in, the Kansas wheat crop would top 8 million bushels, the largest production in six years, but still not up to the levels of 1931.[11]

The End of the Dust Bowl?

Residents of the Southern Plains certainly had cause to celebrate. At last, the cycle of drought had completed its course, or so it seemed. By most accounts, the former Dust Bowl area was making a recovery. One government official said that only about one fourth of the former Dust Bowl area was still experiencing blowing soil. He warned, though, that the next few years would be an important test of whether favorable conditions could keep the dust from returning. The government urged all farmers to continue contour farming and strip farming to help the land recover. It also asked states to set up local soil conservation districts with the help of farmers in each district.[12] If the days of blowing dust became, as that optimistic reporter had said, "rapidly dimming memories," would the lessons learned about soil conservation also be forgotten?

10

The Dust Bowl Legacy

Although the rain brought back life to the prairie, the Dust Bowl remains a significant memory for all Americans. It was a learning experience for the United States, but a lesson that came with suffering. It was a lesson in the dangers of pride and greed. It was a lesson in the delicate balance of nature. It was a lesson that challenged many of the attitudes that Americans had always taken for granted.

Good-bye to Jefferson's "Agrarian Ideal"

President Thomas Jefferson's ideas about the farmer's ability to live off his own land had vanished. Even hard-working farmers found themselves at the mercy of the weather. Until the 1930s and the AAA, farmers never imagined they could be paid not to plant crops. Today, crop reduction subsidies are common.

Back to Old Habits

Once the rains returned, American agriculture again flourished and American farmers again became prosperous. Harvests increased far beyond levels ever seen—even higher than the record-breaking year of 1931. As the 1940s progressed, many countries, including the United States, became involved in World War II. As had happened thirty years earlier, war increased the need for more grain to send to other countries.

As the demand for grain increased, so did the price paid at market. Again, farming was a profitable business, and the more grain a farmer could produce, the more money he could make. Since moisture was plentiful, it was easy for farmers to abandon the conservation techniques they had adopted during the 1930s. Why practice strip farming, when it was more profitable to farm wheat on every available square foot of land? Why bother farming on the contour, when straight rows made it easier to pull the newer, bigger plows across the fields? Why have "perfectly good" land (most of which had been called "submarginal" just a few years earlier) covered with grass, when it could be used for farming?

Soil conservationists became alarmed by what was happening on the Great Plains in the 1940s. It seemed very much like the "plow-up" that had occurred during the 1920s—the one commonly believed to have caused the Dust Bowl conditions. As regional director for the SCS, Howard Finnell had once given the farmers hope that the Plains could again be made productive. He now began to feel that greed was leading farmers to their own destruction. "We are headed into the same conditions that gave us the old Dust Bowl," Finnell warned. "The next Dust Bowl will be bigger and better."[1] Of course, few farmers took him seriously. What could go wrong?

The "Filthy Fifties"

The year 1952 brought a new drought to the Great Plains, and soon, the landscape turned frighteningly familiar. The winter of 1953–1954 brought less than 50 percent of the normal rainfall for much of the nation. The spring of 1954 came with the same kinds of dust storms that had swept the Southern Plains in the 1930s. In a grim reminder of the Dirty Thirties, the decade soon became known as the "Filthy Fifties."

When February 19, 1954, dawned, residents of Syracuse, Kansas, had to check their clocks to tell if it was really morning. According to Reverend Jerald Bushman, "At noon, it's darker than midnight. We ordinarily have the street lights, but the dust cuts out nearly all their light."[2] An article in *U. S. News and World Report* estimated that over one million acres of farmland in Texas, Oklahoma, Kansas, New Mexico, and Colorado had been severely damaged by the loss of topsoil, and that another migration from the Plains was beginning.[3]

Even with the drought of the 1950s, farmers showed no commitment to practicing soil conservation. In Scott City, Kansas, county officials met to discuss the enforcement of a 1937 dust-blowing law. Once again, farmers who did try to stop their fields from blowing were frustrated by the lack of concern shown by their neighbors.[4] The drought ended in early 1957, but not before serious damage had been done to the land.

Still More Dust

In the 1970s, there was more land in cultivation than ever. Some of it was former Dust Bowl acreage, which, until the last few years, had been covered by grassland since the 1930s. Another great "plow-up" uncovered millions of acres in 1972. Overseas demand for wheat raised prices as high as $6.00 per bushel.[5] It was a great time to be a farmer. That was, at least, until the rain stopped.

In 1974, drought hit again. By 1976, wind erosion had again damaged over a million acres. The evening of Tuesday, February 23, 1977, brought a dust storm to western Kansas that lasted all night, all the next day, and into Wednesday evening as well. The description sounded familiar: "It was as dark as midnight at noon here, so dark visibility was zero. The fine dust sifted into every nook and cranny, leaving county residents with a massive clean-up job in the storm's aftermath."[6] Luckily, rains later that year settled the dust once again.

Irrigation Not a Permanent Solution

Since the 1930s, farmers have attempted to overcome the problems of drought and dust with irrigation. Irrigation is a common farming technique in much of the former Dust Bowl area, but it is also an expensive measure. Wells deep enough to tap the Ogallala Aquifer require a lot of drilling. Sprinkler systems are even more expensive.

Another concern is the source of the water. According to scientists, irrigation systems that pump from the Ogallala Aquifer are using up the underground water at a rate ten times faster than nature can replenish it. What will happen to farmers dependent on irrigation when their wells run dry?

Continuing Concern

It seems clear that no matter how farmers attempt to deal with the environment, the dry climate of the Great Plains will continue to be a problem. Drought hit the area again in 1988 and 1989, leading to predictions of another Dust Bowl. Fortunately, rains in the summer of 1989 eased the drought, but it was too late to save that year's crop. The summer of 2000 brought more worry. The Dust Bowl area of the 1930s was again reported to be "abnormally dry," with some areas of Texas experiencing "severe" or "extreme" drought conditions. Between July 1, 2000, and August 30, 2000, areas of north Texas experienced a record dry spell of sixty days with no rain. This surpassed the previous record of fifty-eight days, set in 1934 and tied in 1950.[7]

Perhaps the most important lesson for agriculture is that the Great Plains will never truly be under the control of human beings. No matter how farmers try to guarantee a good crop, they will always be taking a gamble against nature. The only "sure bet" is that dry years will happen, and then the spring winds will blow the dry soil. Soil conservation will be popular only in times when the winds threaten to blow the dust.

We Will Remember

Those people who lived through the Great Depression and the Dust Bowl will never forget it. But what about those who were born too late to have seen the black blizzards? How will later generations remember the lessons the Dust Bowl had to offer? It is fortunate that those who experienced the poverty, the pain, and the powder-fine dirt have left some parts of it behind to help us understand.

Artists and the WPA

President Roosevelt believed that artists, like other workers, needed jobs to survive. Therefore, he included jobs for artists in his WPA plan. Today, the works created by those artists are still available. The artwork created by WPA-employed artists included visual arts such as paintings, photographs, posters, and crafts. Performing arts like drama, dance, and music also captured the richness of American culture and expressed ideas about American politics and society. These works provide the most vivid images of life in America during the Great Depression. They also provide images of the Dust Bowl and its residents that serve as a grim reminder of that experience.

This teacher was employed by the WPA's Federal Music Project to teach violin lessons.

The WPA artists had several goals that seem to be present in most of the work they produced. They tried to portray the common people in their homes and at their jobs. They also tried to capture the mood of America in the 1930s, a time when many people struggled in poverty and hunger. A third goal of the artists was to preserve the richness and diversity of American culture. Critics of the WPA program accused the artists of "New Deal propaganda," since much of their work supported the president's relief programs. Still, the main theme running through the WPA-produced

Charles L. Todd and Robert Sonkin recorded the music of fiddler Will Neal at a migrant farm worker camp in California as part of a WPA program to record folk music.

work seems to be the strength and character of the American people as they struggled through this difficult time. Since these works were commissioned by the federal government, they now belong to the American people as a whole.

Visual Arts of the New Deal

Many painters were employed by the WPA to create murals illustrating local and regional history for the public buildings built by WPA construction workers.

New courthouses and post offices were beautified with paintings that showed historical people and events important to the area. American Indian artists also created artworks for post offices and other public buildings. In 1935, a special board was set up by the Department of the Interior to help American Indian artists market their work.

Artists were also employed to create advertising posters for the government to promote programs like the CCC, the WPA, and public health programs. Many of these posters still exist today. The National Archives Building in Washington, D.C., displays many of these artworks, and the National Archives Web site also shows many examples.

Faces of Our Past

Perhaps one of the most famous programs of the New Deal was the FSA/Office of War Information photography project. From 1935 to 1945, thousands of photographs documented the lives of Americans. Photographers like Dorothea Lange, Russell Lee, and Arthur Rothstein traveled the country taking pictures of dust dunes, exodusters in migrant camps, and farmers who worked to save their farms. These photographs showed the grim reality of the Dust Bowl and its residents. They also showed the spirit and courage of people surviving the best they could. Today, the Library of Congress keeps these images in its American Memory collection. The Web site of the Library of Congress displays hundreds of photographs

The WPA employed artists to create posters for government programs, such as the newly created Social Security Board.

that capture the life of ordinary people during the 1930s.

Performing Arts and the New Deal

The WPA also sponsored the work of playwrights and musicians. WPA choreographers staged dance performances. Many of these productions were written to make social comments about America. Some theater productions used headlines of the day as their subjects. These became known as "living newspapers." Other productions introduced people to modern dance.

WPA sponsored performing artists who captured the history and cultural richness of American life. Choreographers created stage productions using folk dance and music of many different ethnic groups to help preserve their cultural heritage. The WPA-funded Federal Music Project recorded the spirituals of African Americans, fiddlers from Middle America, American-Indian songs, work songs, and many other types of music to create a library of American culture for future generations.

Literature and the New Deal

Writers carried on the tradition of transcribing American culture, also. They traveled the country using tape recorders to capture the tall tales, folklore, and oral history of America and her people. They wrote the stories of local and regional history from interviews with many people in all parts of the country.

Other Writers of the 1930s

Of course, WPA arts were not the only ones being produced in the 1930s. John Steinbeck's novel *The Grapes of Wrath,* the story of Okies who left the Dust Bowl, was one of the most influential books of the period. It helped Americans understand the problems of the Dust Bowl refugees. Other writers who used their literature to express the pessimism of the national mood were Richard Wright, James Agee, and Erskine Caldwell. Most of these writers included characters who, like many Americans, were suddenly aware that the "American Dream" had become more of a nightmare.

Other writers of the period wrote for an audience who wanted stories to take them away from the realities of the Depression. Margaret Mitchell's book *Gone With the Wind* was a successful novel of the 1930s. Millions of copies of the book were sold. The western novels of Zane Gray were also popular with audiences who wanted to escape their troubles and read a good story.

Music in the Depression

In addition to the WPA musicians' projects, folk music was popular in most rural communities, where neighbors enjoyed coming together for "barn dances" or other community events. In urban areas, jazz and blues were popular. In the 1930s, opera changed into a more American product. Instead of the Italian or Spanish productions, American composers looked to

American folklore to write songs more people could relate to. George Gershwin's *Porgy and Bess* was adapted from an African-American story, as was a ballet version of *Frankie and Johnny.* Productions like these gave an American flavor to music and theater.

Woody Guthrie's Dust Bowl ballads told stories of life in his home state of Oklahoma and of the Okies who migrated to California. Through his lyrics and music he captured the hope, and sometimes hopelessness, of those who endured the years of dust. Although Guthrie died in 1967, the mood of life in the Dust Bowl lives on in his songs like "So Long, It's Been Good to Know Ya," and "Dust Storm Disaster."

The Spirit of the Prairie Homesteader

From the first days after the passage of the Homestead Act, through the drought of the 1890s, the Dust Bowl, and the occasional drought of today, it has taken a lot of courage to settle on the Great Plains. Many have come and gone, but some of the people who still live there today have dug in their heels and stayed through both good times and bad. Most of these, like Claudene Davis Schmidt, her sister Margaret Davis Harper, and their brother Homer Davis, admit that life in the Dust Bowl was hard, but they would not live anywhere else. Homer wrote a poem to capture the spirit of the homesteaders like his father, H. M. Davis, who settled on the prairie:

The Prairie Pioneer

By Homer Davis

They came, not to make a fortune,
Nor did they come in quest of fame—
But they came to seek a homestead,
And they came to file a claim. . . .
Here they settled on the land,
With cows and pigs and chickens—
Anchored down and took their stand,
And worked to beat the dickens. . . .
The blasting wind in raging might,
Billowed up the rolling dust—
Took your breath and dimmed your sight,
The very Devil in his lust.
But, no storm without an ending,
Brighter days came, by and by—
Happy days, a promise blending,
Like a rainbow in the sky.[8]

★ TIMELINE ★

1803—President Thomas Jefferson acquires the Great Plains for the United States in the Louisiana Purchase.

1806—Zebulon Montgomery Pike leads an expedition into the Louisiana Territory, and describes the Southern Plains as a desert.

1862—Congress passes the Homestead Act, opening up land for settlement.

1889–1895—Drought hits the Southern Plains; Many settlers move out of the area.

1909—Congress passes the Enlarged Homestead Act, allowing homesteaders to acquire larger farms.

1910–1929—Boom of settlement on the Plains; With years of good rain and high prices for grain because of World War I, farmers prosper.

1929—Stock market crash; Great Depression begins.

1931—Record wheat crop on the Plains; Prices drop; Drought begins.

1932—Drought continues; Dust storms begin; Many farmers cannot repay equipment loans, make mortgage payments, or pay taxes.

1933—Dust storms increase; The decade is nicknamed the Dirty Thirties; FDR takes office; Federal work relief programs help many Americans; The AAA gives aid to farmers through payments for crop reduction, cattle buyouts, and crop loans.

1934—The worst period of "black blizzards" begins; Effects of the drought spread to include over 70 percent of the nation.

1935—*April 14*: "Black Sunday" brings in the worst dust storm of the era, a dust cloud that travels hundreds of miles and leads many residents to think it is the end of the world. *April 27*: SCS is established by Congress.

1936—The WPA is formed to give employment to millions of Americans and create public projects to benefit all Americans; Los Angeles chief of police sends patrolmen to stop "Okies" at the state's borders with Arizona and Oregon; AAA is repealed by Congress; It is replaced with the SCDAA.

1937—Soil conservation activities of farmers, submarginal land removed from farming, and shelterbelts of trees result in reduction of blowing soil, although the drought continues.

1938—After a winter with more moisture than the Plains have seen in years, farmers harvest the largest crop since 1932.

1939—The Dust Bowl officially ends, although farmers are cautioned to continue the soil conservation techniques they have been using.

1940s—The next big "plow-up" on the Plains occurs because of fair weather, rising grain prices, and World War II; Soil conservationists warn that the next Dust Bowl may be worse than the last.

1952–1957—Drought again overtakes the Plains; Dust storms return; The decade becomes known as the Filthy Fifties.

1972—Grain prices rise to a record high; More land is now in cultivation than at any previous time in the history of the Plains.

1974–1977—Drought strikes again; Dust storms again sweep the Plains.

1988–1989—Yet another drought and still more dust storms.

2000—Drought conditions in Texas and other areas ruin crops and bring back fears of still more dusty conditions.

★ Chapter Notes ★

Chapter 1. Black Sunday

1. Woody Guthrie, "Dust Storm Disaster" (New York: TRO, 1960, renewed 1963, Ludlow Music, Inc.). Used by permission.

2. Donald Worster, *Dust Bowl: The Southern Plains in the 1930s* (Oxford: Oxford University Press, 1979), p. 18.

3. "Dust Storms Continue," *The Dodge City Journal,* April 18, 1935, p. 1.

4. "Black Pall Made Sunday Day of Fear," *The Dodge City Daily Globe,* April 15, 1935, p. 1.

5. Ibid.

6. James R. Dickenson, *Home on the Range: A Century on the High Plains* (New York: Scribner, 1995), p. 127.

7. Pamela Riney-Kehrberg, *Rooted in Dust: Surviving Drought and Depression in Southwestern Kansas* (Lawrence, Kans.: University Press of Kansas, 1994), p. 28.

8. "No Ceiling to Dust Cloud," *The Dodge City Daily Globe,* April 17, 1935, p. 3.

9. Lawrence Svobida, *Farming the Dust Bowl* (Lawrence, Kans.: University Press of Kansas, 1986), p. 106.

Chapter 2. The Great American Desert

1. Thomas Jefferson, Letter to John Jay, August 23, 1785. Published in Saul K. Padover, *Thomas Jefferson and the Foundations of American Freedom* (Princeton, N.J.: D. Van Nostrand Co., 1965), p. 111.

2. Zebulon Montgomery Pike, "Appendix to Part II." In *Sources of the Mississippi and the Western Louisiana Territory* (Ann Arbor, Mich.: University Microfilms, Inc., 1966), p. 8.

3. Joanna Stratton, *Pioneer Women: Voices from the Kansas Frontier* (New York: Touchstone, 1981), p. 54.

4. Olof Olsson, Letter to C. W. Weinberg, September 11, 1869. Published in David P. Greenberg, *Land That Our Fathers Plowed: The Settlement of Our Country as Told by the Pioneers Themselves and Their Contemporaries* (Norman: University of Oklahoma Press, 1969), p. 98.

5. Pamela Riney-Kehrberg, *Rooted in Dust: Surviving Drought and Depression in Southwestern Kansas* (Lawrence, Kans.: University Press of Kansas, 1994), p. 6.

6. Donald Worster, *Dust Bowl: The Southern Plains in the 1930s* (Oxford: Oxford University Press, 1979), p. 83.

7. "The Grasslands," *Fortune,* November 1935, p. 65.

8. Worster, pp. 83-84.

9. David P. Greenberg, ed., *Land That Our Fathers Plowed* (Norman: University of Oklahoma Press, 1969), p. 97.

10. James R. Dickenson, *Home on the Range: A Century on the High Plains* (New York: Scribner, 1995), p. 132.

11. Ibid., p. 133.

12. Economic Research Service, United States Department of Agriculture, "A History of American Agriculture 1776–1990: Farm Machines and Technology." n.d. <http://www.usda.gov/history2text4.htm> (June 24, 2000).

13. Worster, p. 89.

Chapter 3. Drought and Depression Set In

1. Pamela Riney-Kehrberg, *Rooted in Dust: Surviving Drought and Depression in Southwestern Kansas* (Lawrence, Kans.: University of Kansas Press, 1994), p. 21.

2. Donald Worster, *Dust Bowl: The Southern Plains in the 1930s* (Oxford: Oxford University Press, 1979), p. 92.

3. Riney-Kehrberg, p. 21.

4. David A. Shannon, *20th Century America: The Twenties and Thirties,* 3rd ed. (Chicago: Rand McNally, 1974), vol. 2, pp. 148–152.

5. Riney-Kehrberg, pp. 22–23.

6. "A New Racket," *Liberal News,* June 1, 1932, p. 1.

7. "Many Are Using Horses," *Liberal News,* May 14, 1932, p. 4.

8. Wayne G. Broehl, Jr., *John Deere's Company: A History of Deere & Company and Its Times* (New York: Doubleday, 1984), p. 503.

9. "Cut in Teachers' Salaries," *Liberal News*, April 28, 1932, p. 1.

10. George Casey, interview by author, July 25, 2000.

11. Ann Marie Low, *Dust Bowl Diary* (Lincoln: University of Nebraska Press, 1984), p. 49.

12. Claudene Davis Schmidt, letter to the author, July 17, 2000.

13. Ruth Townsend, interview by author, August 14, 2000.

14. Claudene Davis Schmidt, letter to the author, July 17, 2000.

15. Jean Gregg, interview by author, July 25, 2000.

Chapter 4. Living With the Dust

1. Margaret Bourke-White, "Dust Changes America," *The Nation*, May 22, 1935, p. 597.

2. Pamela Riney-Kehrberg, *Rooted in Dust: Surviving Drought and Depression in Southwestern Kansas* (Lawrence, Kans.: University of Kansas Press, 1994), pp. 25-26.

3. "Dust Storm is a Test of Husband's Love," *Dodge City Daily Globe*, April 16, 1935, p. 1.

4. "Notes From the Dusty Front," *Dodge City Daily Globe*, March 18, 1935, p. 1.

5. Claudene Davis Schmidt, letter to the author, July 17, 2000.

6. George Casey, interview by author, July 25, 2000.

7. Margaret Davis Harper, letter to the author, July 17, 2000.

8. Clifford R. Hope, Sr. "Kansas in the 1930s," Kansas State Historical Society. March 14, 1997. <http://www.kshs.org/perspect/ks1930s.htm> (May 13, 2000), p. 3.

9. Claudene Davis Schmidt, letter to the author, July 17, 2000.

10. Betty Ann Riley, letter to the author, July 7, 2000.

11. Lawrence Svobida, *Farming the Dust Bowl* (Lawrence, Kans.: University of Kansas Press, 1986), pp. 137–138.

12. Pamela Riney-Kehrberg, pp. 32–33.

13. "Make Masks for Dust Zone," *Dodge City Daily Globe*, April 27, 1935, p. 1.

14. "Wear Masks is R. C. Plea," *Dodge City Daily Globe*, April 30, 1935, p. 3.

15. "Health in Dust," *Dodge City Daily Globe,* April 16, 1935, p. 1.

Chapter 5. Dusty Communities

1. Margaret Davis Harper, letter to the author, July 15, 2000.

2. Margaret Bourke-White, "Dust Changes America," *The Nation*, May 22, 1935, pp. 597–598.

3. "Notes from the Dusty Front," *Dodge City Daily Globe*, March 18, 1935, p. 1.

4. "Twelve Relief Workers Join Janitorial Staff," *Dodge City Daily Globe*, April 16, 1935, p. 1.

5. "Shorten Class Periods to Fight the Dust," *Dodge City Daily Globe*, April 17, 1935, p. 6.

6. "Notes from the Dusty Front," *Dodge City Daily Globe*, March 18, 1935, p. 1.

7. "Eager for Washed Air," *Dodge City Journal*, April 15, 1935, p. 1.

8. Lawrence Svobida, *Farming the Dust Bowl* (Lawrence, Kans.: University of Kansas Press, 1986), p. 132.

9. Travis Gregg, interview by author, August 23, 2000.

10. Claudene Davis Schmidt, letter to the author, August 23, 2000.

11. "Rabbit Drives," *Dodge City Journal*, January 17, 1935, p. 2.

12. "Estimates Rabbit Population at 484 a Section," *Dodge City Journal*, April 11, 1935, p. 1.

13. Bourke-White, p. 597.

14. Svobida, pp. 135–136.

15. "Editor Says Dust Not New," *Dodge City Daily Globe*, April 26, 1935.

Chapter 6. Washington Lends a Hand

1. David A. Shannon, *20th Century America: The Twenties and Thirties,* 3rd ed. (Chicago: Rand McNally College Publishing Co., 1974), vol. 2, p. 158.

2. Ibid., pp. 163.

3. Ibid., pp. 169–170.

4. George Roberts, interview by author, September 4, 2000.

5. James R. Dickenson, *Home on the Range: A Century on the High Plains* (New York: Scribner, 1995), p. 135.

6. Shannon, p. 177.

7. "Youth Plan Latest New Deal Project," *Dodge City Daily Globe*, June 26, 1935, p. 1.

8. Shannon, p. 191.

9. New York City Federal Theatre Project, *Sing For Your Supper.* Quoted from National Archives and Records Administration. "A New Deal for the Arts: Work Pays America," March 27, 1997. <http://www.nara.gov.exhall/newdeal/work1.html> (September 9, 2000).

Chapter 7. Washington Helps the Farmers

1. Lawrence Svobida, *Farming the Dust Bowl* (Lawrence, Kans.: University of Kansas Press, 1986), p. 78.

2. Ibid., p. 77.

3. "AAA Cattle Report Gives New Drought Damage Data," *Dodge City Journal*, February 28, 1935, p. 1.

4. "AAA Director Asks Big Vote on Crop Plan," *Dodge City Daily Globe*, May 4, 1935, p. 1.

5. Svobida, pp. 86–87.

6. "It Happened One Day," *Time*, May 27, 1935, p. 18.

7. "Dragons' Teeth," *Time*, May 13, 1935, p. 15.

8. Franklin D. Roosevelt, "The Drought: A Fireside Talk Broadcast from Washington, September 6, 1936," *Vital Speeches of the Day*, Vol. 2, October 7, 1935–October 1, 1936, p. 765.

9. "AAA: New Program With a Coat of Constitutional Whitewash," *Newsweek*, March 7, 1936, p. 12.

10. Ann Marie Low, *Dust Bowl Diary* (Lincoln, Nebr.: University of Nebraska Press, 1984), pp. 103–106.

Chapter 8. The Great Migration

1. Robert Geiger, "Panhandle Farmers Defy the Drought and Dust," *Dodge City Daily Globe*, April 15, 1935, p. 6.

2. Margaret Bourke-White, "Dust Changes America," *The Nation*, May 22, 1935, p. 597.

3. Donald Worster, *Dust Bowl: The Southern Plains in the 1930s* (Oxford: Oxford University Press, 1979), p. 49.

4. "California: Golden State Insists on Golden Passports," *Newsweek*, February 15, 1936, p. 15.

5. "Transplanting," *Time*, May 6, 1935, p. 17.

6. "Palmer, Alaska—I Love Alaska," 1998. <http://ilovealaska.com/alaska/Palmer> (August 24, 2000).

7. Claudene Davis Schmidt, letter to the author, July 15, 2000.

Chapter 9. Working With Nature

1. Wayne Gard, "America's Desolate Acres," *Current History*, June 1935, p. 259.

2. Harold Ward, "Erosion: The Nemesis of Soil," *The New Republic*, March 18, 1936, p. 162.

3. Ibid., p. 162.

4. Donald Worster, *Dust Bowl: The Southern Plains in the 1930s* (Oxford: Oxford University Press, 1979), p. 213.

5. Lawrence Svobida, *Farming the Dust Bowl* (Lawrence, Kans.: University of Kansas Press, 1986), p. 75.

6. "Contour Land Saves Water," *Dodge City Daily Globe*, June 26, 1935, p. 1.

7. George Roberts, interview by author, September 4, 2000.

8. "The National Grasslands Story," United States Forest Service, n.d., <http://www.fs.fed.us/grasslands/text.htm> (November 1, 2001).

9. Pamela Riney-Kehrberg, *Rooted in Dust: Surviving Drought and Depression in Southwestern Kansas* (Lawrence, Kans.: University of Kansas Press, 1994), p. 23.

10. "Southwest Travels Road to Recovery at a Rapid Pace," *Garden City Daily Telegram*, June 22, 1938, pp. 1–2.

11. "Eight Million Bushels of Wheat in Territory," *Garden City Daily Telegram*, July 19, 1938, p. 1.

12. "Dust Bowl Smaller, But a Critical Period Lies Ahead," *Garden City Daily Telegram*, July 16, 1938, p. 1.

Chapter 10. The Dust Bowl Legacy

1. Donald Worster, *Dust Bowl: The Southern Plains in the 1930s* (Oxford: Oxford University Press, 1979), p. 226.

2. Reverend Jerald Bushman, "Dust Storm Brings Darkness at Dawn," *Syracuse Journal*, February 26, 1954, p. 1.

3. "Is Dust Bowl Coming Back?" *U.S. News and World Report*, March 5, 1954, p. 35.

4. "Stronger Laws Asked by County Officials to Combat Soil Erosion," *Garden City Telegram*, March 16, 1954, p. 1

5. Worster, p. 233.

6. "Storm Darkens Skies, Damages Crop Land," *Syracuse Journal*, March 2, 1977, p. 1.

7. "Dust Bowl 2000," *Kansas City Star*, August 30, 2000, p. C1–2.

8. Homer Davis, "The Prairie Pioneer," 1977. Used with permission of the author.

★ Further Reading ★

Books

Andryszewski, Tricia. *Dust Bowl: Disaster on the Plains.* Brookfield, Conn.: Millbrook Press, 1993.

De Angelis, Therese. *The Dust Bowl (Great Disasters: Reforms and Ramifications).* New York: Chelsea House Publishers, 2001.

Ganzel, Bill. *Dust Bowl Descent.* Lincoln: University of Nebraska Press, 1984.

Hesse, Karen. *Out of the Dust.* New York: Scholastic Press, 1997.

Low, Ann Marie. *Dust Bowl Diary.* Lincoln: University of Nebraska Press, 1984.

Porter, Tracey. *Treasures in the Dust.* New York: HarperCollins, 1997.

Riney-Kehrberg, Pamela. *Rooted in Dust: Surviving Drought and Depression in Southwestern Kansas.* Lawrence: University of Kansas Press, 1994.

Stanley, Jeff. *Children of the Dust Bowl: The True Story of the School at Weedpatch Camp.* New York: Crown Publishing Group, 1993.

Worster, Donald. *Dust Bowl: The Southern Plains in the 1930s.* New York: Oxford University Press, 1979.

Magazines

Chasan, D. J. "Will the Dunes March Once Again?" *Smithsonian*, December 1997, pp. 70–79.

Howarth, William. "The Okies: Beyond the Dust Bowl." *National Geographic*, September 1984.

"The Once and Future Dust Bowl." *Discover*, April 1997, p. 16.

★ Internet Addresses ★

Discovery Communication, Inc. "The Day of the Black Blizzard." *Discovery Channel Online*. 1996–1997. <http://www.discovery.com/area/history/dustbowl/dustbowl1.1.html>.

Library of Congress. "America from the Great Depression to World War II: Photographs from the FSA-OWI, 1935-1945." *American Memory Collection*. 1998. <http://memory.loc.gov/ammem/fsowhome.html>.

Library of Congress. "Voices from the Dust Bowl: The Charles L. Todd and Robert Sonkin Migrant Collection 1940-1941." *American Memory Collection*. January 8, 1998. <http://memory.loc.gov/ammem/afctshtml/tshome.html>.

National Archives and Records Administration. *A New Deal for the Arts*. March 27, 1997. <http://www.nara.gov/exhall/newdeal/newdeal.html>.

WGHB Educational Foundation. "Surviving the Dust Bowl." *The American Experience*. PBS Online WGHB. 1998. <http://www.pbs.org/wgbh/amex/dustbowl>.

★ Index ★